D0356115

Managing Legal Risks in Early Childhood Programs

How to Prevent Flare-Ups from Becoming Lawsuits

Managing Legal Risks in Early Childhood Programs
How to Prevent Flare-Ups from Becoming Lawsuits

Holly Elissa Bruno
Tom Copeland

Teachers College
Columbia University
New York and London

www.redleafpress.org
800-423-8309
Saint Paul
Minnesota

Library Resource Center
Renton Technical College
3000 N.E. 4th Street
Renton, WA 98056

344.032712 BRUNO 2012

Bruno, Holly Elissa.

Managing legal risks in
early childhood programs

Published simultaneously by Teachers College Press, 1234 Amsterdam Avenue,
New York, NY 10027, and by Redleaf Press, 10 Yorkton Court, Saint Paul,
MN 55117

Copyright © 2012 by Teachers College, Columbia University

All rights reserved. No part of this publication may be reproduced or
transmitted in any form or by any means, electronic or mechanical, including
photocopy, or any information storage and retrieval system, without
permission from the publisher.

Library of Congress Cataloging-in-Publication Data

Bruno, Holly Elissa.
    Managing legal risks in early childhood programs : how to prevent flare-ups
from becoming lawsuits / Holly Elissa Bruno, Tom Copeland.
        p. cm.
    Includes bibliographical references and index.
    ISBN 978-0-8077-5377-4 (pbk. : alk. paper)
        1. Day care centers—Law and legislation—United States.   2. Early childhood
education—Law and legislation—United States.   3. Child care services—Law
and legislation—United States.   I. Copeland, Tom. II. Title.
    KF2042.D3B78   2012
    344.7303'2712—dc23   2012024398

ISBN 978-0-8077-5377-4 (paperback)

Printed on acid-free paper
Manufactured in the United States of America

19   18   17   16   15   14   13   12   8   7   6   5   4   3   2   1

We dedicate this book with gratitude to Holly Elissa's partner, Richard Thomas Harrison, and to Tom's wife, Diane, for their graciousness in accepting the hours we devoted to the book and not to them.

Contents

Acknowledgments

We thank: Ronni Rowland and Brandy Ward for invaluable research and assistance; early childhood education colleagues Kay Albrecht, Sharon Bergen, Cindy Croft, Deb Crowl, Bess Emanuel, Deb Habedank, David Heath, Charlotte Hendricks, Angela Jensen, Kyla McSweeney, Lisa Polk, Diane Purcell, Roz Quest, Linda Sakrismo, Susan Snider, Teri Talan, Holly Turner, Ken Wood, and Reva Wywadis and insurance agents Liz Downs, Debe Marofsky, Rex Dachenbach, Chel Buttchen, John Oliver, and Don Morgan for insightful feedback; Marie Ellen Larcada for being our patient editor at Teachers College Press.

Introduction

"Can My Child Care Program Be Sued?"

If you have ever asked yourself this question, you are not alone.

The threat of being sued strikes fear into the hearts of administrators, directors, owners, board members, and teachers in early childhood programs. Few program directors can afford an attorney; fewer administrators have legal backgrounds. Nonetheless, as educators, you make daily decisions with legal ramifications.

You may be called upon to make snap judgments with potential serious legal consequences in situations like these:

- Baby Elisha's dad careens into the program, appearing intoxicated, insisting he will drive his baby home.
- Iraqi War veteran Andrew, interviewing for infant room teacher, shrugs off his coat, revealing he has one arm.
- Teachers' aides who posted a provocative video of themselves on YouTube insist they are exercising their First Amendment rights.
- The Park family wants to include their 12-year-old daughter, Jin Hee, on the Authorized List for picking up their toddlers.
- Lead teacher Roderick's classroom performance is excellent, but his gossiping and negativity are destructive.
- Teacher Gertrude's pungent body odor interferes with her job performance.

Worrying about being sued can interfere with your professional judgment, making decisions harder. This book can help you do the following:

- Prevent and manage problems with legal consequences
- Reduce the risk of a lawsuit
- If your program is sued, assist in preparing a strong defense

By setting a framework for how you can legally and ethically re-solve conflicts with families and staff, we hope this book will reduce the stress that comes with worrying about legal matters. Confidentiality, hiring and supervising staff, health and safety, child abuse and neglect, and discrimination are among the topics.

We identify, analyze, and offer solutions to potential legal dilem-mas using case studies to address the legal and ethical issues involved. Sample policies, procedures, and best practices will help you gain con-fidence in resolving each challenge.

We hope you will be relieved and informed, challenged and as-sisted, in creating ways for you and your center to avoid potential lawsuits.

This book is directed primarily at those working in out-of-home settings caring for young children. However, family child care provid-ers will find much of the content relevant, particularly if considering working at out-of-home early childhood education programs at some point.

This book was a collaborative project, but we each took primary re-sponsibility for writing five chapters. Holly Elissa wrote Chapters 1, 4, 6, 8, and 9. Tom wrote Chapters 2, 3, 5, 7, and 10. Although our writing voices are different, we hope this enhances, rather than distracts from, the book's readability.

THE LIMITS OF THIS BOOK

This book offers practical advice in an accessible manner. But it is not a substitute for a lawyer. We neither assume you are an expert on legal issues nor that you want to be a lawyer!

Disclaimer: The information is made available in this book with the understanding that the authors and publisher are not engaged in rendering legal or other professional advice. If you require legal or pro-fessional assistance, engage the services of a competent professional. This book was published in 2012. Federal and state laws referred to in this book may change over time. State laws can also vary from state to state. Before taking action you may want to consult with an attorney to learn about the specific laws in your state.

Managing Legal Risks in Early Childhood Programs

How to Prevent Flare-Ups from Becoming Lawsuits

Knowing the Right Thing to Do

Guidance from Legal History, Legal Theory, and Brain Research

Imagine the tears tumbling down toddler Clarence's cheeks as he presses his cherubic ebony face into the window glass of his classroom, searching, heartbroken, for his teacher who is late (again). What would be the right thing to do? Hold Clarence's habitually tardy teacher accountable? Take her through the steps of progressive discipline? If she continues to arrive late, tell her "You're fired"?

As early childhood leaders, when we focus on high standards of quality care and education for children and families, we know the right thing to do. Clarence deserves our best.

Knowing the right thing to do legally isn't always so clear, however. Stacks of musty judicial decisions, changing state and federal regulations, plus dog-eared handbooks of policies and procedures can complicate our decision making. Teachers, parents, and community members, often with opposing views, expect us to champion their side. Being able to see the merits in each group's position and foresee their outrage if decisions don't go their way can turn our decision-making path into a mine field.

This book clarifies how to make intelligent choices, both to prevent legal difficulties and address what can't be prevented. Practical tips on "how to think like a lawyer" follow in Chapter 2. There you will learn in concrete terms how an attorney is likely to assess everyday challenges that early childhood professionals face. In that chapter we start with "first things first": making decisions, both reasoned and compassionate, that put us in good stead legally.

Before we continue, let's be clear on expectations: This book is not a substitute for your seeking legal advice. We are not acting as your attorneys, nor are we giving legal advice. However, we believe we can offer useful information to support you in the challenging decisions you make daily.

ARE YOUR DECISIONS "FAIR ENOUGH" OR "NO FAIR!"?

Leaders are judged on the fairness of their decisions. Unpopular decisions, if fair, garner respect, albeit grudgingly. Decisions seen as unfair land you in a bog of discontent. Disgruntled employees or families, like a dog with a sock in its mouth, will shake their heads ferociously all the way to court.

We all know what's fair. Or do we? Is it fair to withhold the truth from preschooler Anna's ailing grandmother, while telling Reginald's thicker-skinned father the blunt reality? Is it fair to discipline teacher Ted for being late while excusing Mei Lin for lateness because her relatives are visiting?

If your answer is: "*It depends* on the situation and individual circumstances," you are in the majority of early childhood decision makers (Bruno, 2012). If your answer is: "Treat everyone the same way. What's fair for one is fair for all," you are in line with the majority of executives and (56%) of men (Myers et al., 1998). However, in our caring profession, you may be seen as "having ice in your veins" and out of touch with people's feelings. If so, you can expect resistance to your decisions.

Definitions of fairness differ. To gain a sense of what courts have held to be "fair," let's look into legal history.

Definitions of Fairness from a Legal History Perspective

To understand what's fair, we need to time-travel to 12th-century England. Imagine you are a judge presiding over the Law Court in the sheep-grazing countryside of feudal England. William, who rents his farmland from a local lord, appears before you, asking that he and his family be permitted to stay on the property.

Everyone knows the law: Tenants must pay their rent to the landlord on time. Failure to pay on time will result in forfeiture of the land. Although William's rent was due on April 15, he paid his rent on April 20. Should he forfeit his property because he knowingly broke the law? What seems fair to you?

The judge decided: "Forfeit the property. Quit the land." William had failed to obey the law. Breaking the law led to a clearly stated consequence: forfeiture. The judge did not take into account William's personal circumstances. The judge used a logical, "letter-of-the-law" approach consistent with his other decisions: Lawbreakers suffer consequences. Everyone could expect the same treatment: "What's fair for one is fair for all."

William's neighbors, however, were outraged. "No fair!" they cried. They knew William had paid his rent on time for 5 years. William was an upstanding citizen and responsible father of 11. He was late with this payment, even after traveling day and night, because spring rains had washed out the bridges William usually crossed to deliver his rent. The community festered over the judge's "cold-hearted" decision. Word reached the king.

To head off situations like this, the king took action. He created a Chancery Court in London, where controversial cases like William's could be appealed (Kerly, 1890). If justice was not served by the legal decision, the case could be reviewed by a different standard of fairness. The king appointed the ecclesiastical member of his cabinet to preside in this new appeals court to add a tone of moral "rightness" to the position. The king's appointed adjudicator was called "chancellor," not "judge."

The chancellor of this new court could take into account all the individual circumstances of the aggrieved. If the chancellor decided the facts in the case were compelling, the Law Court's ruling could be overturned.

The equity chancellor overturned the Law Court's decision and returned the property to William for having made a "good-faith effort" (traveling night and day) in the face of an "act of God" (flooding). Acting on William's claim, the chancellor used an artful decision-making process, drawing from an alternative definition of fairness. To this day, phrases like "good-faith effort" and "act of God" have been passed down from original Equity Court decisions.

From reversals like those in William's case, the "spirit of the law" became legitimized as an official decision-making process (Blackstone & Cooley, 2003). Decisions could be equally well made on a case-by-case basis, taking into account each person's individual circumstances.

Letter-of-the-Law Standard for Fairness

Are you finding yourself more in alignment with the reasoning of the Law Court judge or the case-by-case analysis of the equity chancellor? Which definition of fairness do you most often use? Are you still thinking: "It depends"? Let's take a closer look at each standard.

With the letter-of-the-law process, fairness equals applying the law the same way to every person (Blackstone & Cooley, 2003). Individual circumstances are immaterial. The "law is the law." Consistency is the hallmark.

Letter-of-the-law decisions ensure evenhanded justice. People know what to expect: decisions are predictable. Letter-of-the-law decision makers argue that "the floodgates will open" if the law isn't enforced uniformly.

Letter-of-the-law decisions are made by weighing the pros and cons of each option. When making budget decisions, you may find this process appropriate:

1. List pros of the situation objectively.
2. List cons objectively.
3. Analyze the list: Which side has more substantial factors?
4. Make a logical decision favoring the weightier side.

Letter-of-the-law decisions make a leader's life easier by being:

- Expedient (made quickly)
- Defensible (based on measureable facts and figures)
- Impartial (no favorites)
- Consistent (evenhanded)

At times, this process works well. Administrators, pressed by an onslaught of choices, find the objective approach useful. When a leader makes an "impartial" decision, he or she can decide quickly without considering the complexity of human emotion.

Leaders base their decisions on established policies and procedures, and, in "following precedent" or upholding tradition, promote stability. Expectations are met.

THINK ABOUT IT

When has your letter-of-the-law decision been right for the situation? When has another letter-of-the-law decision backfired? What accounted for the difference?

When do you use the letter-of-the-law process? When you do, you meet one standard for fairness. However, you may be faulted for not taking a more interpersonal approach, the "spirit-of-the-law" process.

More often than not, an impartial decision will be challenged. Letter-of-the-law decisions are resisted by individuals who feel their personal circumstances were not considered. An administrator may hear complaints that he or she failed to ask everyone's opinion before deciding.

Spirit-of-the-Law Standard for Fairness

While letter-of-the-law (legal) decisions are expedient, spirit-of-the-law (equitable) decisions require reflection time. Legal decisions call upon our rational processes (IQ); equitable decisions require us to use both rational and emotionally intelligent (EQ) or integrated processes (addressed later on in this chapter in the section on emotional intelligence in decision making). Discerning which type of decision-making process is more appropriate calls for a leader's intellectual savvy and skillful ability to perceive the underlying emotional dynamics.

When you make a spirit-of-the-law decision, you take into account the "totality of the individual's circumstances" (Blackstone & Cooley, 2003). You look for the root cause of the problem in order to make a decision tailored to each individual situation. Most likely you will consider the following:

- What is the person's explanation?
- Were there mitigating circumstances? Did anything "beyond the person's control" cause the unwanted result?
- What is the person's overall track record? Has she been reliable and dependable?
- Is this a "first offense" or part of a pattern of inappropriate behavior?
- What effect will this decision have on the person and her family?
- What will help the person change for the better?
- Will this decision promote community harmony?

Because of their history and origin in the Court of Equity, spirit-of-the-law decisions are also called "equitable" decisions. Equitable decisions require evaluating each person on a case-by-case basis as a unique individual. No "one-size-fits-all" template works.

Leaders who make spirit-of-the-law decisions are seen as caring individuals. Parents and family members share their concerns with such a leader, knowing their viewpoints will be fully heard. Spirit-of-the-law decision makers are often loved and admired for their wisdom and compelling interpersonal skills. However, letter-of-the-law decision makers may label equitable decision makers as "pushovers."

THINK ABOUT IT

When has your spirit-of-the-law decision been right? When has another spirit-of-the-law decision backfired? What accounted for the difference?

IS ONE DECISION-MAKING PROCESS FAIRER
THAN THE OTHER?

Leadership requires maturity. Knowing when to use compassion and when to strictly follow the rules is a judgment call we make in the moment. Most situations, like individuals, are complex.

Neither decision-making process is superior to the other. However, people passionately argue that their definition of fairness is superior. You are judged by how well you judge. Awareness of your favored process and/or definition of fairness is empowering.

If you do not have to make an immediate decision, step back to theoretically apply both processes to the situation. Ask yourself: Which process and decision feels "right" to me? Does my conscience cause me to cringe when I use either of these processes? Our sense of rightness deepens with each decision we make (Gladwell, 2005). Sometimes, second-guessing yourself is more debilitating than productive. Ask yourself: "Is my decision fair enough?" If your answer is "yes," move on. Another decision awaits your attention anyway. (See Appendix: Helpful Websites.)

Later in this chapter, we will look at what takes place on a cellular level when we make decisions. You may find this neurobiological information liberating or at least useful. Knowing that our "gut" decisions are often our best decisions builds trust in our own judgment. That trust and our underlying confidence make decisions less ponderous to make.

One final word: Although you may see yourself as preferring one definition of fairness over another, know that both processes are available to you. If a letter-of-the-law decision doesn't sit well with your conscience, be open to making a more "equitable" decision. If your highly interpersonal decision feels off, ask what you would do if you were that 12th-century judge. Would his letter-of-the-law decision feel fairer to you? Knowing your options helps as legal dilemmas break open.

Here is another process emerging from our legal history that will help you as a decision maker: *due process*. Using due process enhances the fairness of your decisions.

DUE PROCESS MODEL OF FAIRNESS

If you tell Clarence you are serving pizza for lunch, but instead substitute chicken fingers and broccoli, you expose yourself to Clarence's scowling: "No fair!" Even with the best of reasons, your changing of an established expectation will be met by resistance from children, their families, and employees.

If you tell your staff you are instituting a No Babysitting policy, you may find an angry group of teachers in your face. Why is resistance to change, even if the change is well intended and necessary, inevitable?

The answer lies in a legal process originating in the 14th Amendment to the U.S. Constitution: due process (Strauss, n.d.). Due process consists of:

1. *Notice*: telling people about a decision before you finalize it
2. *Right to a hearing*: giving people a chance to share their ideas with you before you make a change

We become invested in our expectations. Clarence expects pizza, not chicken, and certainly not broccoli. Teachers rely on extra income from babysitting. Teachers expect policies and procedures to stay the way they were when they were hired.

THINK ABOUT IT

What is your most recent experience with due process? Have you failed to provide due process and experienced resistance? When is due process not appropriate?

Resistance to Decisions

Neila Connors (2003) provides these statistics on how teachers respond to change:

1. Five percent (5%) of teachers embrace change immediately
2. Ten percent (10%) dig in their heels and resist, arguing, "If it ain't broke, don't fix it" (or don't count on me to fix it!)
3. Twenty-five percent (25%) slowly adapt and change
4. Sixty percent (60%) respond, "I will wait and see what's in it for me."

Think of an innovation you were excited about making. What percentage of your staff responded with as much enthusiasm as you? In fact, recall times when your decisions hit a brick wall with your constituents.

Your decision-making process, whether letter or spirit of the law, may explain why some people were upset with you. However, the majority of times our decisions are resisted, lack of due process is the reason.

Notice

People need ample time to change. Although inevitable, change is threatening. Have you heard the adage: "An expectation is a resentment waiting to happen"? We become invested in the way things are. Leaders need to make sure their constituents do not feel blindsided by change. "Notice"—telling people in advance what you are thinking before you make a change—is essential (Strauss, n.d.). Written notice provides documentation that you are following due process.

Here's an example: You are considering instituting a professionalism policy to prevent inappropriate behavior in public, including online. Tell your staff you are concerned about possible misuse of online, social networking sites. Remind them of your confidentiality policies, designed to protect the privacy of children, families, and employees. Lay out in writing the policy and procedures you are considering to make sure online networking sites are used appropriately.

Notice is providing all pertinent information before you change the policy. Most newspapers post notices of upcoming changes in your community. Before holding a person to a temporary restraining order, the court must serve notice. Clarence needs to know before lunch is served that the menu has changed. Notice is a component of transparency.

Right to a Hearing

Like darkness and dawn, notice is followed directly by the right to a hearing. People affected by a change need freedom to voice their concerns and ask questions. In short, people need to be heard.

Often through the hearing process you find new ideas that temper the change you were thinking of making. One teacher might ask: "Is texting between my boyfriend and me considered to be public?" Another may pose: "What I do on my own time is my right! You can't tell me what I can say online." In that case, your revision of the proposed policy lets teachers know you have heard them. Politicians hold hearings before enacting legislation.

When you introduce a controversial policy, you can expect resistance. You will hear all kinds of complaints when you grant that right to a hearing. You do not need to use any or every suggestion. Letting your constituents "have their say" is adequate for due process. In the end, no one can claim: "You never told me that!" or "You never asked my opinion!"

The expectation of due process is deeply embedded in our culture. Just as equitable decisions can take longer to make, providing due process lengthens the time before your decision can take effect. However, the decision will more likely be received well. People will have no surprises.

HOW RATIONAL ARE OUR DECISIONS?

Throughout the centuries, judges have held us to standards like "what would a *reasonable man* do" in the same situation? Courts look to see if we have a "rational basis" for our decisions. In criminal cases, juries must find defendants guilty "beyond a *reasonable* doubt." Reasoned decisions are respected.

Because the rational, objective decision-making process is favored by the courts, letter-of-the-law decisions appear to be safer. Certainly the documentation of objective facts and figures will hold sway with courts. Like people, courts are not quick to change. Courts uphold prior decisions in order to follow precedent (*stare decisis*). Even when scientific research suggests that the court should revise and update standards, courts resist.

Recent research in the new and burgeoning field of neuroscience (the study of how our relationships affect every cell in our bodies) poses a challenge. Thanks to the functional MRI (*f*MRI), neuroscientists can look into the inner workings of the brain. This research strongly suggests that following a letter-of-the-law, rational process of decision making does not produce our best decisions. In fact, our wisest decisions may be those gut decisions that utilize all of our brain's resources, not just our IQ.

Paying attention to this developing research helps us understand what neurobiological processes drive our wisest decisions. (See Appendix: Helpful Websites.)

Rational Decisions and the Brain

The human brain has "grown up" in its own way. A comparatively recent development in our brains is the orbital frontal cortex (OFC), or our "executive function." Located just beneath our foreheads are brain pathways allowing us to assess situations and weigh decisions. In short, the OFC enables us to think like an executive.

This prefrontal cortex is associated with intellect or IQ. IQ is, in turn, associated with "hardheaded" thinking processes. Our IQ is tested as we proceed through our school years. Our IQ score predicts in many cases if and where we will go to college, whether we are perceived of as "bright" or "dim," and certainly whether we qualify for MENSA, the exclusive organization requiring an IQ in the 98th percentile or above.

Gut Decisions or "Thin-Slicing"

Malcolm Gladwell (2005) challenged the assumption that using the executive function of our brains leads to the best decisions. Gladwell proposes instead that we make our best decisions by "thin-slicing." He says: "Thin-slicing is not an exotic gift. It is a central part of what it means to be human. We thin-slice whenever we meet a new person or have to make sense of something quickly or encounter a novel situation. We thin-slice because we have to, and come to rely on that ability..." (p. 43). (See Appendix: Helpful Websites.)

Thin-slicing is akin to making a "gut decision." Gilkey, Caceda, and Kilts maintain that our best decisions are not made through our rational, executive function (2010, p. 23). Instead, wise decisions utilize all of our brain resources, including those identified with emotions and intuition:

- *Insula*: is necessary for emotional processing.
- *Anterior cingulated cortex*: enables us to make decisions based on our experience with and evaluation of prior experiences.
- *Superior temporal sulcus*: allows us to anticipate other people's emotions and thoughts by reading their and our own sensory stimuli.

Using all of our brain resources is also known as "EQ" or "emotional intelligence" (Goleman, 1995). EQ, the ability to read people as well as we read books, draws on our intuition, intellect, sensory capacity, and other internal processes.

The more mature we are emotionally, the greater the library of stored experiences we have from which to generate intuitive decisions. In fact, Cozolino in *The Neuroscience of Human Relationships* (2006) argues that as we grow in experience, the more streamlined our decision making becomes.

Irrational or Fear-Driven Decisions

One of the brain's earliest-developing components, the amygdala gland, is lodged deep inside the head. The amygdala served our forbearers well, as they survived outdoors under threat of wild-animal attack and were at the mercy of weather extremes. The amygdala alerts our bodies that we are in immediate danger. If we encounter a snake in our path, we halt. If we see a child in danger, we rush in to help.

The amygdala responds before we stop to think. Before we know it, our heart is pounding, breathing is shallow, and our mind is hyperfocused on stopping or escaping from the threat. At the command of our amygdala, adrenalin spurts through our system, making us feel "pumped" to do what we have to do in the crisis.

Here's the problem: the amygdala functions as it always did. If we are threatened, even if the threat is an interpersonal slight or a traffic jam, we can hit overdrive. The common term for this is "amygdala hijack" (Goleman, 1995). We shift into "fight-or-flight" response even if the danger is not real or substantial. To the amygdala, a threat is a threat: adrenalin is triggered.

Road rage is an example of an overreacting amygdala. The triggered driver literally becomes combative, ready to fight. If you have been in a car with a driver having a road-rage attack, or if you have been that driver, you have witnessed or experienced an amygdala hijack. To complicate the experience, "coming down" from an amygdala hijack takes time. Meanwhile, we may say or do something we regret.

Perhaps this is what judges are wary of: irrational decisions based in fear rather than in strength. One thing is clear: If at all possible, don't make a decision when you feel threatened. In panicky times, your brain is only partially operative. The amygdala, a primitive force, blocks other brain functions.

Wait until you can catch your breath and see through to the other side of the danger. When you feel like your professional self again, you will be able to make a decision that courts will uphold.

Cozolino (2010) advises: "As we mature, our amygdala matures with us. It seems to be much more gentle with us and is much less activated by anxiety." Gladwell says we can teach ourselves to make better snap-decisions. Awareness of the amygdala's power to overtake us is useful to our decision-making process.

CODES OF ETHICS

Given these complexities of making fair and wise decisions, keeping perspective is necessary. Early childhood professional organizations offer us guidance through codes of ethics. The gold standard is the National Association for the Education of Young Children's (NAEYC)

Library Resource Center
Renton Technical College
3000 N.E. 4th Street
Renton, WA 98056

Code of Ethical Conduct and Statement of Commitment (2005). This comprehensive nine-page position statement offers guidelines for responsible behavior in the daily practice of working with young children and their families. The Code consists of a series of core values (statement of commitment), ideals (aspirations of workers in the field), and principles (guidance for workers in resolving ethical dilemmas).

The NAEYC Code has also been endorsed by the Association for Childhood Education International and adopted by the National Association for Family Child Care. In 2006, NAEYC adopted a Supplement to the Code for early childhood program administrators that outlines additional core values, ideals, and principles to assist administrators with ethical dilemmas. The NAEYC Code was not intended to address every specific situation you may encounter in your program. But its standards are an excellent place to start when you face an ethical question.

There are other early childhood codes of ethical conduct. The National Association of Child Care Professionals has a one-page Code of Ethics that is very general and does not address particular ethical dilemmas. Head Start has a one-page Standards of Conduct. Because the NAEYC Code is the most thorough tool, we will refer to it throughout this book.

Our "ethical responsibilities, the things that the good professionals will always do or always refuse to do, are clear-cut and spelled out in the NAEYC Code of Ethical Conduct" (Feeney & Freeman, 2000, p. 39). Feeney adds: "Ethical dilemmas, however, are situations in which two or more different responses can be defended by NAEYC's Code." In that case, Feeney encourages decision makers to "distinguish between personal preferences and morality and professional ethical responsibilities."

In some situations, distinguishing between a personal preference and professional ethical responsibility is, as Feeney says, easy. Parents may believe spanking a child is effective at home. However, if parents ask us to spank their child, we say "No" and discuss why. In other, more complex ethical dilemmas, knowing the right thing to do may not be as clear-cut.

Case Study: Reporting Suspected Abuse

A recently hired teacher, Annalise, clearly upset, says, as a mandated reporter, she must report baby Tia's mother for harming her child.

Annalise points to red marks on baby Tia's back as clear evidence of abuse. Which of the following should you do:

- Call the Department of Social Services immediately?
- Call Tia's mother to ask about the red marks?
- Decide whether to report or not based upon what the mother says?
- Co-report the incident with Tia's mom?

Tia's mom explains she used "coining," a healing tradition passed down in her Hmong family, to help Tia recover from a budding cold. Mom adds proudly: "Tia is so much better this morning! We are so relieved."

What effect does this information have on your mandated reporting decision? What is the right thing to do? Do you apply letter-of-the-law principles and report the mother regardless? You may decide to counsel the mother that although you understand her good intentions and appreciate her cultural heritage, other mandated reporters, like her pediatrician's office, might not. When we take into account spirit-of-the-law and letter-of-the-law factors, our decision becomes more complex. Fortunately, this is where the Code of Ethics offers guidance.

NAEYC's Code begins with Core Values, those principles that constitute the essence of our professional responsibilities. When we take these principles to heart, we become more confident and competent at thin-slicing our decisions. We agree to:

- appreciate childhood as a unique and valuable stage of the human life cycle;
- base our work on knowledge of how children develop and learn;
- appreciate and support the bond between the child and family;
- recognize that children are best understood and supported in the context of family, culture, community, and society;
- respect the dignity, worth, and uniqueness of each individual (child, family member, and colleague);
- respect diversity in children, families, and colleagues;
- recognize that children and adults achieve their full potential in the context of relationships that are based on trust and respect (*NAEYC Code of Ethical Conduct*, 2005).

With core values, we can make a more informed and intuitive decision about baby Tia and her family.

Your Choices or Checklist for Making Wise Decisions

What is fair and right is not always clear. What makes sense to you may not make any sense to another. We become invested at a cellular level in our ways of making decisions. This chapter, in spelling out where definitions of fairness originate, both historically and neurobiologically, offers perspective as you make your next decision. As you face that decision, you may consider the following:

- What matters most?
- What does our Code of Ethics require?
- How can I make the fairest and wisest decision for children, families, staff, the program, and my conscience?

Picture Clarence, the child in your care who needs your best self. In his eyes, you will find inspiration to do the right thing.

2 Acting Ethically While Reducing the Risks of a Lawsuit

Although it's true that anyone can sue you for almost anything, it rarely happens. And when it does, you will be relying on an attorney to represent you. What we hope to do with this book is to help you take steps and make decisions that will reduce the chances of a lawsuit, as well as reduce the chances that the other side will win. To do that, we first present a theoretical framework for thinking about how to approach conflicts that could lead to a lawsuit if not handled properly, followed by a four-step prevention checklist.

A THEORETICAL FRAMEWORK TO REDUCE THE RISKS OF A LAWSUIT

Our theoretical framework involves incorporating legal, regulatory, and ethical standards into your daily decisions. Be assured that you don't have to be a professional juggler to handle all of these tasks at one time!

We are assuming that you are a decision maker (whether as an administrator, center director, classroom teacher, family child care provider or someone who strives to be one). As such, you must take action when faced with a problem or conflict. Your decision can avert a crisis or cause a parent to hire a lawyer to prepare a lawsuit against your organization. Even the failure to make a decision can be a decision that may have serious consequences. This is a lot of responsibility. But we believe that most readers won't shy away from responsibility if they have the proper knowledge and tools.

To approach a potential legal or ethical issue, first you need to know the limits under which your decision making should operate. Here we introduce three standards that you can incorporate into this process. The first two involve legal restrictions and early childhood regulations and contracts that you are required to follow. The third is an ethical commitment that is voluntary.

Obey the Law

Many state and federal laws apply to your program, including antidiscrimination laws, child abuse laws, the Americans with Disabilities Act (ADA), IRS payroll tax laws, state wage and labor laws, and privacy and 1st Amendment laws. Yes, these are a lot of laws to consider!

Your responsibility is to understand and follow these laws. The consequences of failing to do so can be severe. You, your center, and your staff can be fined, in some cases severely enough that your center may have to close. You or your staff could face jail time for committing child abuse or neglect.

On the other hand, compliance with the law helps protect you and your center from lawsuits. Yes, there is some good news! Clear policies and procedures go a long way toward showing your compliance with the law. For example, new-hire interview forms that show your program asks consistent questions of each candidate can deflect accusations of discrimination in the hiring process.

Comply with Early Childhood Regulations and Government Contracts

You and your early childhood program are also required to follow a variety of state regulations. These include child care licensing rules and mandated reporting standards. If your program receives funding from federal, state, or local government agencies (Head Start, subsidized child care program, Pre-K, Quality Rating and Improvement System programs, Child and Adult Care Food Program, etc.), you must comply with the rules in the contracts you sign. Failure to follow some of these rules can result in losing your job and your ability to work with children elsewhere. State agencies can also kick your center off their program, fine your center, or shut it down.

Let's say a child tips over a bookcase and is injured in your program. At the time of the injury, your program is out of compliance with a state child care licensing rule because you don't have the proper number of staff present. If your compliance failure is related to the injury, parents can use this against you in court.

In this case, judges are likely to rule that your program is more negligent than if the proper number of staff were present with the child. If your only licensing violation was a lack of proper immunization records, then this is unlikely to have any bearing on this case in court.

Since compliance with state regulations can go a long way toward protecting you and your program from a lawsuit, your goal should be to have an impeccable licensing-inspection record (even if you think that some rules are trivial!). Look at each regulation that your program follows as potential evidence that can be used in your defense in a lawsuit.

Failure to follow the rules of child care subsidy programs and other government-funded programs can also affect the quality of your center and reduce your ability to serve children in need.

Relationship with Licensing. It's important to have a positive, professional relationship with your licensor. In particular, you want to keep your licensor informed of conflicts with parents of the children in your program. Contact your licensor in the following situations:

1. A parent threatens to sue you if you don't do what she wants.
2. You are about to terminate a family from your program (or a family is ending your agreement) and the parents are upset and angry.
3. You are having continuous and unresolved arguments with a parent.

The purpose of contacting your licensor is threefold:

1. To go on record about a problem that could in the future lead to a parent making a complaint to licensing
2. To request and document your licensor's input on issues
3. To build a trusting and professional relationship that may help you in later difficult situations

Here's an example of what you might want to say when making a call to your licensor:

> Hi, Irene! I'm calling about a parent in our program, Mrs. Cutts, who is very upset that her child's teacher will not tell her the name of the child who bit her child two days ago. We have explained our procedures for how we deal with biting and have given her another copy to take home. She is still upset and insists that we must reveal the name of the child, despite what our policy says. Please put a note in our files that we had this conversation in case the parent later files a complaint.

If Irene has heard about your conflict with Mrs. Cutts before the parent calls to complain, your call can make a difference in how she might handle the complaint. Licensors who know about such conflicts are more likely to give your program the benefit of the doubt if Mrs. Cutts later complains that your program violated a rule.

Although a licensor's visit can be as welcome as a trip to the dentist, licensors share the same goal as you: quality care and education for children. Building a cordial, collegial relationship with your licensor leads to your having an ally outside your program who is dedicated to the well-being of the children. Asking for your licensor's input on sticky problems gives you additional perspective, especially when you are closely involved in the issue.

On some occasions, you and your licensor may have a different interpretation of licensing rules. When this happens, feel free to ask the licensor's supervisor for clarification. If necessary, you may want to ask the state licensing office to provide additional input.

Mandated Reporting. State laws dictate that you are a mandated reporter of child abuse and neglect. As such, you face serious consequences if you or your staff fail to meet your responsibilities. If you are in doubt about the circumstances in which you should be reporting, do not hesitate to ask your state child-protection agency or your licensor for clarification.

Let's say one of your staff, Elana, sees a parent picking up her child in a vehicle without an appropriate child restraint. Should Elana report the parent to child protection? Should Elana first call the police? If you are not sure, find out what to do.

Let's say that a child in your program tells her teacher, "I fell down last night while Mommy was putting me to bed." You are not sure if this should be reported, so you call child protection. They tell you not to report it. After any conversation with child protection, make a note of your conversation: date, name of person you talked with, your question, and their answer. By following the directions of these agencies you can reduce your liability should a parent make a complaint later against your program about child maltreatment. (For a state directory of mandated reporting rules, see Appendix: Helpful Websites. For a discussion of how to respond to accusations of child abuse or neglect against your program, see Chapter 5.)

State Child Care Subsidy Programs. Some child care centers that serve state-subsidized families may not know all of the rules of the program. May you charge subsidized families a registration fee or require full payment a week in advance? May you charge private-pay families more than subsidized families? Sometimes a worker for the subsidy program and you will interpret a rule differently. If so, you may want to talk to the supervisor and seek clarification. If necessary, ask for a written statement of his or her position.

The general point of this section is to reinforce the message that you want your program to be in compliance with all state child care regulations and contracts. Doing so can make a difference in reducing the risk of a lawsuit.

Set and Follow High Ethical Standards

We believe it's not enough just to follow the law and regulations in the field of early childhood education. This third leg of our theoretical framework involves a commitment to following ethical standards that will benefit children, families, staff, and the broader community you serve. Following ethical standards is voluntary. But this does not make them any less important than obeying the law and meeting your obligations under child care regulations and government contracts.

We are also aware that the child care licensing standards in many states are inadequate; some barely cover more than basic health and safety rules. We recommend that child care centers seek out and meet the highest-quality standards in the field. This can include accreditation through NAEYC or the National Early Childhood Program, as well as participation in Quality Rating and Improvement System (QRIS) programs. A commitment to ethical and quality standards will help reduce the risks of child injuries and parent lawsuits. Compliance with higher standards of quality (even if your program is not accredited) can also be used to defend yourself if your program is sued.

As we mentioned in the previous chapter, we encourage early childhood professionals to heed NAEYC's Code of Ethics and strive to establish and maintain best-program practices. A commitment to these ethical standards can help your program balance your legal responsibilities with your keen desire to do what is best for the children in your care. You don't want following the law to be your ultimate goal. Helping children grow and their families thrive is always paramount.

Although the NAEYC Code of Ethics is often not specific when confronting particular ethical situations, we believe it is useful as a guide to treating everyone with the greatest respect.

Case Study: Handling Different Religious Beliefs

Melissa and Lance Puckett are talking with you during a prospective parent interview about their child Diane. At one point Melissa says, "Since we are Jehovah's Witnesses, we do not celebrate Christmas or birthdays. We do not want our child exposed to this in your center, so we ask that you not celebrate these occasions."

How should you respond to this request?

Legally your program cannot discriminate against families because of their religious beliefs. (It's a violation of Title VII of the Civil Rights Act of 1964.) So, you would be violating federal law if you said, "I'm sorry but we cannot enroll your child because you are Jehovah's Witnesses."

But the law does not require you to change your program's religious practices to meet the needs of parents. So you are free to pray with children, teach Bible stories, and/or observe Chanakuh. You can also celebrate birthdays. You are also free not to follow these observances.

Child care licensing or mandated reporting issues do not appear to apply in this situation. What about the ethical issues?

The first principle in the NAEYC Code of Ethics is "Above all, we shall not harm children. We shall not participate in practices that are emotionally damaging, physically harmful, disrespectful, degrading, dangerous, exploitative, or intimidating to children" (P-1.1. "P" refers to the Code's principles.).

The Code also says your program cannot discriminate based on the religious beliefs of families (P-1.3) and that your program should develop a "relationship of mutual trust" and "create partnerships" with the families you serve (I-2.2. "I" refers to the Code's ideals.). Elsewhere the Code calls on you to respect the "dignity and preferences" of each family and to learn about its "beliefs" and "customs" (I-2.5). (The Head Start Standards of Conduct also shun discrimination based on religion [45 CFR 1304.52].)

Given these ethical standards, is it appropriate for you to suggest to Diane's parents that she be taken to another classroom during Christmas and birthday celebrations? What about telling the Pucketts that you will notify them ahead of time when there will be such celebrations so that they can keep Diane away from your program on those days? What about eliminating the celebration of all holidays with religious connotations and not celebrating birthdays?

The answer to the first question may be clear to you that this would be inappropriate, even if the parent agreed with the idea. But the answer to the second question is not so clear. The age of the child could influence your decision. Some programs have decided that the best answer to the third question is "yes." Although this choice puts an end to special traditions, the choice ensures that no child or family is put in an uncomfortable position.

Try not to look at ethical standards as rigidly proscriptive. They should be seen as a helpful tool, a commonsense guide. At a minimum, ethical standards should encourage you to talk with the family about their beliefs. Explain your program's policies with regard to religious holidays and birthdays. This conversation can be an opportunity for you to learn more about Jehovah's Witnesses and what your program can do to accommodate them in other ways. In the end, you can tell the Pucketts your program will not change its policies about religious holidays and birthdays. By being respectful and thoughtful in your discussions with the parents about how to meet the needs of their family, you should be able to come to a mutual understanding about how to handle their request.

Making decisions that are legal *and* ethical is your best protection against a lawsuit. And it's the right thing to do! Ultimately, it's also in the best interests of children. If you turn down Melissa and Lance with a negative comment about their religion, you are risking a lawsuit. If you are ready to enroll Diane into your program without discussing how you will handle her parent's wishes, you are not acting in the best interests of the child or the family. This failure to create a partnership could later create misunderstanding and conflict that might cause the parents to think that your program is discriminating against them.

SELF-PROTECTION CHECKLIST

How should you incorporate these guidelines into the daily operation of your program? Following is a four-point self-protection checklist that you can use to anticipate problems and help you avoid conflicts and lawsuits.

Incorporate Legal and Ethical Standards into the Goals of Your Organization

Organizations that set high standards are more likely to meet them than those that don't set such standards. We recommend that you start with an institutional statement of commitment to follow legal requirements as well as professional and ethical standards. Such a statement might read:

> The ABC Child Care Center is committed to upholding our legal, professional, and ethical responsibilities to the children and families we serve and the workers we employ. We are committed to following all state child care licensing standards and mandated reporting standards for child abuse/neglect. We are also committed to following the professional and ethical standards of the National Association for the Education of Young

Children's Code of Ethics (Revised 2005) and the Code of Ethical Conduct (2006). Copies of all licensing rules and ethical standards are available from the director.

Ask yourself: Has our center committed itself to antidiscrimination policies? Have we adopted the NAEYC Code of Ethics (or the codes of ethics of other professional organizations), and discussed the Code in detail with all staff? If so, staff will feel better prepared to respond appropriately to the Puckett's request.

Recognize Potential Legal Issues Before They Arise

Think ahead about what could go wrong: parent or staff lawsuits, injuries to children, property damage, or complaints to licensing. Many experienced administrators are all too aware that any of these possibilities could involve a legal conflict. But there may be other circumstances that are not so obvious that could result in legal action: staff members give out names of other child care programs to parents when your program can't accommodate them; another child care program director calls and asks for your opinion about whether she should hire a person who used to work for you; or a parent passes out flyers in your parking lot about an upcoming political rally.

Even if you were a lawyer, you may not be able to spot every potential legal conflict ahead of time. Don't lose sleep over this! But you want to be informed and keep up with what is happening in the field and how the laws are changing. Talk to colleagues from other programs and attend legal workshops/webinars. Sign up for "Google Alerts" (do a search for "child care") that allow you to track news (including legal conflicts) in the early childhood field across the country.

If you are a program director, speak to a lawyer several times a year, or as often as you can afford to, about steps your program can take to reduce the risks of a lawsuit. If you can't afford to pay a lawyer directly, ask a lawyer to be on your program's board of directors to serve as your legal counsel. By anticipating legal conflicts before they occur, you will be better prepared for the worst.

Establish Preventative Policies and Procedures

One of the best ways to reduce the risk of a lawsuit is to have program policies and procedures in place that can help prevent legal conflicts. They can also help in your defense if you are sued. Here are the key components that will ensure this.

Develop and Follow Written Policies and Procedures. Written policies and procedures, although essential, mean little unless you model and follow them! The NAEYC Code of Ethics says, "We shall follow all program policies" (P-3B.1). Conduct an annual review with staff to evaluate how well your organization is doing this. If you aren't following a policy, start doing so or get rid of it. Failure to follow your own policies can make you more liable in a lawsuit.

We recommend that your program's policies include an antidiscrimination policy. Here's an example: "The ABC Child Care Center gives equal treatment and access to our program and to our current or prospective employees without regard to race, gender, color, religious creed, national origin or ancestry, medical condition, ethnic group orientation, age, disability, marital status, pregnancy, or sexual orientation."

You may want to use the experience with the Pucketts as an opportunity to review your policies and discuss how you would handle this situation.

Maintain Accurate and Up-to-Date Records. When a lawsuit occurs, one of the first things lawyers want to see is a copy of your records that may pertain to your case. Such records could include children's files, parent contracts, personnel records, minutes and decisions of the board of directors, and tax records. Missing records can hurt you by reducing the amount of evidence you can use in your defense.

As the Head Start adage says, "If it isn't documented, it didn't happen." Simple, concise, and clear documentation does not have to be long or intricate. Make sure you list the essentials of who, what, when, and where. Rarely do you need to document why. Just reference the policy, procedure, or practice that is at issue. For example, when you write up your conversation with the Pucketts, state who was present, what the issue was, key points made and/or agreed upon (bullets are fine), and when the discussion happened. You do not need to write up how you felt or why you were concerned. Let the facts speak for themselves.

Respect Confidentiality. Most of the records your organization keeps are confidential. Make sure you identify who is authorized to see such records and that you enforce this rule. Parents expect your organization to keep all information about their family confidential. Your organization's privacy policy should explain your legal obligations to share information with government officials as well as your commitment to keep everything else confidential, unless there is parental permission. The NAEYC Code of Ethics prohibits the disclosure of children's records (P-2.12). Head Start expects programs to establish confidentiality policies concerning information about children, families, and staff members. If you do release private information, a parent can sue your program.

Imagine that the Pucketts decide to enroll their child in your program and agree to keep their child at home during Christmas and birthday celebrations. What if another parent asks you why Diane is never present during these days? Sharing that the Pucketts are Jehovah's Witnesses breaks confidentiality unless the Pucketts have given you written permission to share this information. You can tell the parent, "Diane's parents choose to keep Diane at home and that's all I can share with you about this." For a complete discussion about privacy and confidentiality, see Chapter 7.

Stay Objective and Act Reasonably. The field of early childhood education is one where emotions are an integral part of the daily work that we do. However, where the law or child care regulations are involved, some emotions can be an impediment. Taking things personally is rarely helpful, even if your feelings are hurt temporarily. You may need to take a few moments (or days!) to regain your professional perspective. When problems develop, take an unbiased, objective approach. You don't want to take sides in a dispute between staff based on your personal feelings. When a parent is upset about your late-pickup policy, you want to be reasonable if the parent has some special circumstances that might excuse her violation of your policy. However, you don't want to set a precedent because the parent complained loudly in front of other parents.

You may personally have had a negative experience with Jehovah's Witnesses or you may not like the fact that Lance Puckett raised his voice while demanding you enroll Diane. Regardless of the fact that your buttons are being pushed, your responsibility is to respond professionally as you discuss options for how your program might meet the family's needs.

Document and Report "Just the Facts." When a problem does arise in your program, keep in mind the potential for a lawsuit. Carefully document what happens. If a parent slips and falls while visiting her child at lunchtime, start a file on the incident. (*Note*: Write up the incident even if the parent doesn't complain of being injured.) Your licensor may have a standard accident report you must use, or you can get one from the NAEYC. Write down what the parent said at the time. Did anyone witness the fall? Have them document what they saw and heard. When the parent later calls you to talk about her medical bills, keep a record of your conversation.

If another parent tells you next week that she knows that the parent who fell was drinking that morning, write down what she tells you and ask her to sign your notes. Put the date and time on each note you put in the file. When writing notes, record the facts (who said what and when), not your feelings at the time ("I felt awful that the parent fell down and wondered if somehow I was to blame."). Do not hesitate to document everything; more records are better than fewer records.

When you do record your conversation with the Pucketts, make a note of what they requested and how you responded. Use quotation marks around statements that you remember in detail. You can record that Lance raised his voice, but don't write how you felt as a result.

Give Respect to Others. The NAEYC Code of Ethics calls on us to "Respect the dignity, worth, and uniqueness of each individual (child, family member, and colleague)." Respect matters whether you are enforcing your program's rules or giving a performance evaluation to a staff member. When a parent tells you she lost her job and can't pay her fee this month, show her respect even if you plan to terminate services. If you say to the parent, "I don't know how we can keep this center open when parents can't pay their bills," you demean the parent and create unnecessary ill will.

Respecting everyone also means being consistent in how you treat others. If in a performance evaluation you are going to deduct points for one employee who rarely offers constructive suggestions at staff meetings, you should deduct similar points for all other employees who do the same. Consistency is common sense, but it also can quell charges of favoritism.

Thanks to our Constitution, everyone has a right to practice his or her own religion or practice no religion at all. If you overhear your staff talking about the Pucketts and making fun of their religion, step in to stop the negativity. Use this as an opportunity to educate staff about respecting differences. If you fail to do this and the opinions of staff get back to this family, you could face unnecessary conflicts down the road.

The more you can promote a trusting relationship with parents (and this starts with treating them with respect), the less likely it will be that parents will sue you (even if they have a valid claim).

Honor Civil Rights. Federal law prohibits discrimination based on age, disability, national origin, race, color, religion, and sex. (See Title VII of the Civil Rights Act of 1964.) The NAEYC Code of Ethics adds marital status/family structure and sexual orientation in cases of staff hiring and firing (P-3C.8) and, in the area of discrimination against children, it adds medical condition (P-1.3). Your state or local government may have added additional protections, such as status with regard to public assistance. Your program can add its own civil rights protections even if your state law does not mandate it.

As states enact different laws about the rights of immigrants, civil rights protections based on "national origin" may be affected. This may put you in both a legal and ethical dilemma. If your state law requires you to report undocumented individuals, and many of your families are, you will have to decide what your stand will be. Will you report undocumented families or will you find a way to continue to offer care and education to their children?

Understand Your Role in Your Organization. The legal structure of your child care program can affect how you respond to legal matters. If your program is incorporated as a not-for-profit, the final legal responsibility for decisions made by anyone in the organization lies with the board of directors. If you are a director or teacher in this organization, you are an employee of the board. As such, the director may want to seek out help from the board when faced with a tough problem (whether to terminate a staff member or not, for example) before making a decision. Board members should be aware of their potential legal liability for decisions made by staff. See Chapter 10 for a discussion of directors' and officers' insurance.

If you own your for-profit center, you alone have the final legal authority for all decisions made by staff. You are responsible to no one else when making decisions. This means you take on all liability as well. Because of the legal exposure in this situation, you may want to establish a regular relationship with an attorney, as well as purchase adequate liability insurance.

Seek Legal Help When Necessary

There may be times when you need professional legal assistance. If you are not sure how the law applies to your center, you may need clarification so you can make a decision. For example: Your staff has been working to try to provide appropriate care for a child with autism for the past month. You believe your center has done everything it can to accommodate this child, without success. You are about to tell the parent that she should look for care elsewhere, but you are worried the parent may make a complaint because she has been loudly insistent that your center must care for her child.

What should you do if the Pucketts insist your program must enroll their child and stop celebrating Christmas and birthdays? If you are unsure of your legal rights, advise the Pucketts that you need to clarify your legal responsibilities in this situation. You can say, "I'm not clear about how our center should respond to your request. I'm going to consult with our licensor and attorney and I will get back to you as soon as possible."

When to Contact an Attorney. Sometimes you can't avoid hiring a lawyer. You've done everything you can to reduce risks and avoid a lawsuit against your child care center. You follow all the laws, maintain a clean licensing record, have clear policies, communicate effectively with parents and staff, and make a point of going the extra mile to treat everyone with dignity and respect. So far, so good!

Does this mean your child care center will never by sued? Unfortunately, no. In the end, you cannot prevent someone from starting a lawsuit. Whether that person will win his or her lawsuit is an entirely different matter. In the meantime, however, you must deal with the frightening reality of being sued.

If you are sued, there are many situations where you won't need to look for an attorney because your insurance policy will provide legal assistance. You don't want to hire an attorney only to find out later your insurance policy would have covered you. Therefore, whenever someone is suing you, first contact your business-liability insurance agent. (See Chapter 10 for a discussion on insurance.)

If a parent or staff person *threatens* to sue your center, it may not be necessary to talk to an attorney. If there is the potential for a claim against your center because of an injury or a staff termination, you should be reporting this to your insurance agent to find out if you are covered. If not, then it's best to wait to see if you are sued before hiring an attorney. If your insurance policy doesn't cover you and you are nervous about the threat of a lawsuit, there is nothing wrong with consulting an attorney to advise you.

If a lawyer representing a parent contacts your center, contact your insurance agent immediately. Do not talk with a lawyer who is representing someone who might sue, or is suing, your center. As child care workers, you are in a caring profession, taught to trust others. You may be tempted to try to solve problems informally or think you can explain to the lawyer what happened and why it's not the fault of your center. Don't try. A lawyer who contacts you is not your friend, no matter how reasonable he or she may sound (remember, the authors are both lawyers!). Because a lawsuit can put your center in serious financial jeopardy, you don't want to take any chances.

Here are some situations where you may want to consult an attorney:

- A police officer or a child-protection worker shows up at your center and wants to talk to you about a parent complaint that one of your staff inappropriately touched a child. In this situation, you definitely want to speak with an attorney.
- You receive a licensing report that indicates your center violated several licensing rules, resulting in a fine of $5,000. Consult an attorney if you want to challenge the licensor's interpretation of the rules.
- A parent leaves your program owing a lot of money. You have tried unsuccessfully to resolve the problem with the parent. You are considering whether to take the parent to small claims court. (To reduce the likelihood this will happen again, rewrite your contract to require payment in advance.)
- One of your employees is badmouthing your organization on her Facebook page. You have discussed the matter with the employee, explained why this is a violation of your organization's policies, conducted a staff meeting to discuss these policies, and given the employee a warning. The employee continues posting negative comments about your center. Before firing this person, you may want to consult a lawyer to make sure you are following all the proper steps to reduce the chance of an employee lawsuit later. (If your center doesn't have a social media policy, now is the time to write one.)

Susan McDonald, a parent who is a delight to be around, comes to you after her child fell off a swing and suffered a minor cut on her leg. The doctor bill is $500 and Susan asks if you will pay the bill. She says she doesn't want to talk to an attorney and will be happy if the bill is paid. Although it may be tempting to make this problem quickly go away by paying Susan's bill, it's not so simple. What if the cut becomes infected later and there are additional medical bills? Can you have Susan sign a statement saying that she will not ask for additional money and will not sue you? What if the child sues you when she becomes of age because her leg never properly healed, and this affects her ability to work?

What once appeared to be a problem with a simple solution is now complicated. First turn to your insurance agent to handle the medical bill and any parent claims. Do not try to prepare a statement for the parent to sign that will prevent her from suing you later. This can be used against you later as an admission of fault.

Finding an Attorney. Many child care centers, particularly small ones, have had little, if any, contact with attorneys. You may not know how to find one and you may be reluctant to hire one because of the cost. Sometimes problems can be solved without legal assistance, through the use of a mediation service. Your community may have a nonprofit mediation service that will bring both sides together to try to resolve a problem through informal discussions. Both sides must voluntarily agree to participate, and any agreement reached cannot be enforced by a court. The cost of using a mediation service is very inexpensive. To find out if there is such a service in your area, contact your local United Way or Google "mediation service" and the name of your state. Consider adding a dispute resolution provision in your enrollment agreement that requires matters in dispute to be submitted to nonbinding mediation before your center or the parent can file a lawsuit. Use of a mediation service can be very useful in working through both large and small disputes.

Hiring a lawyer can be expensive. Some legal services are offered as a flat rate, but most fees are paid based on an hourly rate that can easily exceed $100 an hour. Here are some suggestions for how to find legal help at a reduced cost:

- Many child care centers have a lawyer on their board of directors. This person may be able to give you some limited legal advice, but may not be able to represent your center if it's sued. Hopefully, your attorney can recommend other attorneys who may be able to help you at a reasonable cost.
- Your insurance policies will usually take care of many legal costs. That's one of the big reasons to have insurance.
- Legal Aid is a government program that represents low-income taxpayers. It's unlikely that it will be able to represent your center if you are for-profit, but it may be able to refer you to a lawyer who can help.
- If you believe your center is the victim of discrimination based on race, sex, or religion, you may be able to get legal help from public interest legal organizations at a low cost. Such organizations include: American Civil Liberties Union, National Association for the Advancement of Colored People, Lambda Legal (for gay and lesbian rights), and the National Women's Law Center. (See Appendix: Helpful Websites.)
- Some lawyers offer their services "pro bono" (without charge) as a service to their community. Ask around to find out which law firms offer such help.

- If you live in a city that has a law school, you may be able to get free help if the school sponsors a law clinic. Look online or contact the law schools directly to find out if they have a law clinic. Such clinics usually provide assistance to a narrow population (low-income, Native Americans, prison population, etc.), but it's worth checking out.
- LegalShield, formerly Pre-Paid Legal Services, Inc., provides legal assistance through a network of independent law firms across the country. Members pay a monthly fee and receive legal help at a reduced cost. Services include incorporation, hiring/termination, small claims, landlord/tenant issues, and more. Before enrolling, carefully consider whether your use of these services will justify the monthly fee. (See Appendix: Helpful Websites.)
- Your state or county bar association may offer a lawyer-referral service that can identify which attorneys offer free initial consultations.

Finding the right lawyer for your situation can also be difficult. Most lawyers specialize in a particular type of law, so you want a lawyer who has experience in handling your particular situation. If you are fighting a decision by your licensor to terminate your program, you want an attorney specializing in administrative law.

Choosing an Attorney. Don't be shy about shopping around for a lawyer by talking to two or three before making a decision. Ask about their experiences in handling cases similar to yours. Usually, you will meet with a lawyer for an initial consultation to describe your case, find out what services the lawyer can offer, and decide whether to hire the person or not. Oftentimes, you will not be charged for an initial meeting. Here are some questions to ask:

- How many other cases like mine have you handled? What were the outcomes?
- What do you charge?
- How many hours do you think it will take to resolve my problem?
- How long will it take for you to return my calls?
- Can you give me the names of previous clients I can call as references?

We hope that the framework outlined in this chapter will allow you to approach legal issues with more confidence and reduce the chances you will be sued.

3 Reducing Conflicts with Parents

Using Contracts and Policies Effectively

One of the most important tools you have to help you build parent confidence and trust in your program is your written contract and policies. These are primarily communication tools that can help you establish and maintain a positive business relationship with parents. They can also help you reduce conflicts and reduce the risk of a lawsuit. Only rarely will it be necessary to use your contract as a legal document in court.

A *contract* is a legal, binding agreement between your program and the parent(s) of the child in your care. It spells out the responsibilities of both sides: the child care program's promise to provide child care services and the parents' promise to pay the program for these services. In this chapter we will use the word "contract" and "agreement" interchangeably.

Child care program policies are rules about *how* your program will operate. These can include health and safety policies, a description of your program's mission and curriculum, and policies about naptime, food and nutrition, toilet training, transportation, and so on. There are no rules about how many policies you should have. If you are a new program it might be best to start out with a few policies and add them as the need arises. If your center has been around for a long while and has a stack of policies 10 feet tall, it's time to review them to weed out those that are no longer relevant.

Some child care programs have their contract and policies in one document. Others have separate policies in a parent handbook. Although we recommend that child care programs create two separate documents (to make it easier to enforce the contract), there is no requirement that you do so.

A contract can be verbal or written. Let's say as the director of a child care program, you tell Mrs. Paulson, "I'll care for your child for $250 a week." Mrs. Paulson replies, "I agree," but nothing is put in writing. At the end of the week, she leaves without paying $250. Can you sue Mrs. Paulson in court? Yes, a verbal contract is legally enforceable. However, it will probably be difficult to enforce if she doesn't agree with what you said about your verbal agreement. For example, if Mrs. Paulson says the agreement was for $100, how will you convince the judge that your understanding of the verbal agreement was correct?

Most child care programs use written contracts; sometimes it's a licensing requirement. Those that don't use written contracts may feel that it's easier to proceed informally or they may not know how to create an effective written agreement. Because it's easier to communicate with a written agreement in place, we strongly recommend that all child care programs create written contracts and policies.

A contract will reduce conflicts by spelling out agreed-upon rules and obligations. If either party fails to live up to its responsibilities under the agreement, the contract can be terminated. Either party may then be entitled to sue the other for money damages. Usually this involves a child care program suing a parent for nonpayment of fees, or a parent suing a program for return of fees paid. Note: A discussion about parent lawsuits involving injuries to children is provided in Chapter 5.

Although a contract is a legal document that can be enforced against either party, the primary purpose of a contract (and your policies) is to facilitate communication with the parents in your program. You are not looking to catch parents breaking your contract rules and beating them over the head with it ("You didn't bring the extra change of clothes, so we are terminating you from our program!").

Although the contract sets out rules and expectations, you don't want it to get in the way of your "family-friendly" philosophy. You are always free to bend your rules when you think it's in the best interests of the children and their families. Try to be consistent in how you bend your rules, so as not to be accused of unfair discrimination (be consistently flexible!). In other words, if you are going to allow one parent to be late in paying you because of "special circumstances" (e.g., mother in hospital or father lost his job), you should treat other parents in the same situation in the same way. Don't write down how you will handle "special circumstances" because it's likely that no two situations will be exactly the same.

SETTING YOUR OWN RULES

In thinking about what to put in your contract and policies, we start with the fundamental principle that you are free to run your program however you want. Other than a few restrictions we will cite, you can put whatever you want in your contract and policies. It's your business. If parents don't like your rules, they can choose not to enroll in your program.

You have wide latitude to set your rules:

- You are free to establish your own hours of operation.
- You can care for infants exclusively, or not at all.
- You can run a highly structured program or a very informal one.
- You can serve vegetarian food, choose your own curriculum, or require parents to pay you by the week, hour, day, month, or year.
- And so on.

This freedom to set your own rules should be remembered when conflicts with parents arise. Although you will want to treat parents fairly and ethically, in the end you will make the final decision about your own rules.

RESTRICTIONS ON YOUR CONTRACT AND POLICIES

Despite this freedom, you don't have absolute authority to set whatever rules you want. There are some restrictions you must abide by: antidiscrimination, price fixing, and state early childhood regulations. We live in a society that protects the rights of individuals as well as the health and welfare of children.

Antidiscrimination Laws

Antidiscrimination laws prohibit your program from discriminating against children or parents based on age, disability, national origin, race, color, religion, or sex (we discuss issues of disability in Chapter 6).

Your state or local government may have expanded these rights to prohibit discrimination based on sexual orientation, marital status, or other classifications. Check with your state or county attorney's office for details.

If a person is a member of one of these protected classes, you can still enforce your rules that have nothing to do with a parent or child being in a protected class. So, you can't refuse to enroll Peter because he is a boy, but you can terminate your contract with Peter's parents if they refuse to pay your late-pickup fee.

Here's another example: A child comes to your program each morning with her clothing reeking of cigarette smoke. You could insist that the parents wash her clothes until the smell of smoke is gone; you could wash the clothes at your program; or you could end your contract with the parent. The fact that the parents might be African American, or Muslim, or were born in Cuba does not limit your ability to set or enforce your own rules about cigarette smoke.

However, if a child smells strongly of incense or Indian cooking spices, then the issue could be construed as one of religion or national origin. Even body odor and grooming could be an issue with individuals born outside the United States. You can circumvent these issues by implementing specific policies that do not focus on religion or national origin, but on potential problems these issues can cause (health, social, professional, etc.).

Although your program can establish and enforce almost whatever rules you want, this does not mean we are recommending you set rules that seem arbitrary or unfair. You could charge parents a higher fee if they work for a company you dislike, but we don't think this is a good idea! When you are arbitrary or unfair, for reasons that have little to do with your agency's mission to care for children, parents will react negatively and your program will suffer.

Price Fixing

What's wrong with this scene? You are a center director who calls up your friend Carla Mendoza, the director of another child care center across town, and asks, "Are you planning to raise your rates this fall? We are thinking about increasing our rates by 2%."

If Carla answers your question, you have both broken the law. Really?

It is against the law for child care programs to share information about their parent fees with another child care program. Courts will tend to see this as evidence that you and Carla are attempting to fix your prices higher. It's a violation of federal antitrust laws (specifically, the Sherman Antitrust Act). Your simple discussion about rates can be seen as a probable violation of the law, even if you and Carla don't promise to raise rates or try to convince each other to raise rates.

As you might guess, many child care programs across the country are regularly violating this law! Program directors often talk to each other about potential rate changes over the phone and at workshops or conferences. Sometimes, child care associations may survey their members about their program rates. The occasion where price fixing is most likely to occur is when you are with a group of other center directors.

It's not price fixing unless both parties know they are competitors or if the rate information is public. So, if you and Carla didn't know each other you can call her up and say, "I'm a parent looking for child care. What are your current rates?" In this case Carla can answer your questions and neither of you are violating the law since Carla doesn't know you are a competitor.

Making your rate information public is also not against the law. So, it's not illegal to post your rates on your center's website, advertising flyers, and on Craigslist. If you feel like posting your rates on a flashing neon sign in front of your center, go for it!

But, you still want to know what other competitors are charging. How can you collect this information legally?

- Contact your local Child Care Resource and Referral (CCR&R) agency. It may have rate information (average rates by age group, etc.) that is public.
- Look for rates listed in advertisements by other child care programs through Craigslist and other online classified ads.
- Look for rates posted on competitor websites.
- Ask parents what they paid their last caregiver or what their friends pay for child care.
- Visit other child care programs and collect rate information without revealing that you are a competitor.

Although prosecution of price fixing might be rare, we encourage everyone to avoid discussions about rates with competitors.

State Early Childhood Regulations

Another potential restriction on what you can put in your contract or policies is your state's early childhood regulations.

State licensing regulations typically set out rules about child/staff ratios, teacher qualifications, behavior guidance, activities and equipment, and health and safety standards. Often they will require child care programs to give a copy of the regulations to parents.

State regulations may also identify policies that a program must put in writing, but usually they will not describe the exact language of the policies. Sometimes the regulations can be more specific, such as the Minnesota law that says you must have written permission from parents to transport children (Minn. Admin. Rules, 9502.0405 Subpart 4[E]).

It's common for state regulations to say very little about what must be in the contract between the child care program and parents.

California laws are unusual in that they require the program to include payment provisions, including the basic rate, optional services rates, and due date and frequency of payment (State of California, 2007). In Pennsylvania, programs are required to include in their agreements "the day on which the fee is to be paid" (Pennsylvania Dept. of Public Welfare, 2010).

Check your own state regulations to see how specific they are about what you must include in your contract or policies. Make sure you follow whatever these regulations say. If your state regulations require you to give parents a 30-day notice prior to raising your rates (such as in California), and you fail to give this notice, a parent who challenges your higher rates in court is likely to win. (For a listing of all state child care center regulations, see Appendix: Helpful Websites.)

Child Care Licensors

In Chapter 2 we discussed the importance of maintaining a positive, professional relationship with your licensor. In general, licensors will not get involved in contract disputes you may have with parents. This is because these issues almost always fall outside the realm of state child care licensing rules.

But, if you are having conflicts with parents about your contract or policies, do not hesitate to contact your licensor to keep him or her informed. Doing so can make a big difference in how licensors might handle later complaints from parents. Licensors realize that sometimes parents make complaints about the treatment of their child in retaliation over a contract dispute. If the licensor knows about past contract disputes, she is more likely to ask probing questions of the parent who makes a complaint. When that parent complains that her child's teacher verbally abused her, your licensor may give you the benefit of the doubt.

Here's what you might say to your licensor when you call: "I'm calling about Mrs. Jones, who is likely to be very angry when she receives our termination notice tomorrow. She has been late many times in the last month and is very unhappy about our late-pickup policy. Please make a note in your files that I called today about this parent."

Keep your own record of calls you or your staff make to your licensor. Keep records of conversations you have with parents about any serious problem or conflict. Such records can be extremely helpful later if a parent makes a complaint or files a lawsuit about the care of her child. Previous disputes about a contract can help make your case that the complaint or lawsuit was made in retaliation. This history can be used to argue that the parent's claims cannot be taken seriously.

Ethical Standards

Lastly, we want to consider how ethical standards can affect your contract and policies. In the end, your contract and policies are more about fair-dealing and mutual respect than they are about legal disputes.

As we discussed in Chapter 2, we urge early childhood professionals to follow the National Association for the Education of Young Children's Code of Ethics. One core value of the Code calls upon professionals to make a commitment to "Respect the dignity, worth and uniqueness of each individual (child, family member, and colleague)."

As you establish and enforce your contract and policies with parents, this core value of respect should be at the heart of your interaction with parents.

The NAEYC Code of Ethical Conduct Supplement spells out ideals and principles to help guide administrators' conduct and to assist in resolving ethical dilemmas. It identifies three areas of ethical responsibilities to children, families, and personnel.

One of its principles, under the ethical responsibilities to families, states:

> We shall work to create a respectful environment for and a working relationship with all families, regardless of family members' sex, race, national origin, religious belief or affiliation, age, marital status/family structure, disability, or sexual orientation. (P-2.1)

Notice that this includes sexual orientation and marital status/family structures that are not included under federal antidiscrimination laws.

The Supplement does not directly address what should be in contracts and policies with families, other than saying that programs shall "establish clear operating policies" (P-2.4). It also says programs shall develop clear enrollment policies (P-2.5) that are applied "consistently and fairly" (P-2.8).

Let's now pull together all three legal and ethical standards described thus far by presenting several case studies that will address problems that can arise with parents over your contract and policies.

PAYMENT SCHEDULES

Case Study: Offering Customized Payment Plans

Your child care program's contract states: "Parents must pay the last two weeks of tuition at the time of enrollment." Your mission statement gives notice that you welcome families of diverse backgrounds. However, to date, your families are fairly homogeneous. During your parent interview with Aafiya and Parveen Hijaz, they ask, "Would you accept one week's tuition instead of two? Otherwise, we will be strapped financially." The parents also tell you that they are Muslim and will have certain food requirements for their son. How should you respond?

Legal Restrictions

There are no federal laws that prevent you from setting your own payment schedule. Therefore, you are free to tell the Hijazes whatever you want regarding this. You could insist they pay two weeks in advance, or could set up a payment plan where they pay a little extra each week until the second week of tuition is paid in full.

Since federal antidiscrimination laws do cover religion, you cannot deny care to the Hijazes because they are Muslim. If you offered payment plans to other parents in the past, but refuse to offer a similar plan in this case, you could be accused of religious discrimination. Let's say you offered payment plans to parents up until last year, but stopped because they were difficult to manage. If you refuse to offer a payment plan to the Hijazes, this would not be illegal discrimination because your decision would not be based on their religion.

What about the special food request of the Hijazes? In general, your program is not required by federal law to meet special food requests by parents. If their food request has nothing to do with their religion (they don't want their child to have candy), then you are free to make your own decision. But what if their request is based on their religion? Observant Muslims do not eat pork or other meat that is not halal meat (meat that is slaughtered in a particular manner). In this case, you could not refuse to enroll their child because of their religious food restrictions. But, you are not required to follow the religious practices of your customers. Instead, after agreeing to enroll the child, you could decide whether or not to accommodate the parents' needs. If you chose to serve pork or nonhalal meat, you could serve a meat alternative to the child or make arrangements for the parents to bring their own meat. (The answer would be the same if the parents were Jewish and wanted only kosher food served to their child.)

Early Childhood Regulation Restrictions

Although it's unlikely that your state regulations will have anything to say about payment schedules, read them closely to be sure this is the case. If you are not sure, contact your licensor and ask questions. In most cases, your state regulations would merely indicate that you should put your agreement with parents in writing.

Your state regulations will mirror federal law in outlawing religious discrimination. As a result, you may be able to get further information from child care licensors about how other child care programs have handled similar situations regarding food requests based on religion. Your licensor, however, may or may not have an accurate understanding of state law. If your licensor tells you that you must serve halal food, you can ask her to produce some written authority that supports that position. You can also ask the licensor to get clarification on this point from the state licensing office. Since federal laws are clear that your child care program is not required to follow the practices of a particular religion, it's highly unlikely that a state law will be different.

Ethical Standards

The NAEYC Code calls upon your program not to discriminate based on "religious belief or affiliation." The general intent of the Code and Supplement is for child care administrators to make every effort to work with families to provide appropriate care for their children. They don't give direct guidance about how to handle contract payment schedules, other than they should be clear policies that are applied "consistently and fairly."

Your Decision

It is clear that you cannot refuse enrollment to the Hijaz family because of their religion, but you can insist on them paying the two weeks tuition upon enrollment. You also do not have to serve halal meat. Beyond this, you are free to make your own decision. What other factors should you take into account? Does your program need the full two weeks of tuition upon enrollment? Would changing your rules and allowing this family to make payments over time for the second week of tuition create additional burdensome paperwork? Would it cause other families to want the same flexibility?

There may be other reasons why your program does not want to change its rules. In the end, if these reasons are strong enough, you should tell the Hijazes that you won't change your contract. Listen to their response. If they indicate that it will be extremely difficult for them to enroll their child under your rules, you could negotiate further and agree to an extended payment schedule. If they agree, make a written change to your contract that reflects your new agreement. If you can't come to a negotiated agreement within a short period of time, tell Aafiya and Parveen you are sorry you can't enroll their child and wish them well.

You are also free to decide how to respond to their food requirements. The intent of the Code and Supplement would be to take reasonable steps to try to accommodate the family. Simply saying, "We can't change the food we serve" is not sufficient under the NAEYC Code until you have learned more about the needs of the family and how you might accommodate them. Offering substitutes for meat would be a reasonable compromise.

RATE STRUCTURES

Case Study: Handling the Loss of Funding

Your state legislature has recently cut the child care subsidy payments to your program by 5%. Forty percent of the children in your program are funded by this subsidy. The loss of this income will make it difficult for your program to continue. After a staff brainstorm, you come up with these options:

1. Raise rates for some or all of these families
2. Terminate some of these families
3. Recruit more private-pay families
4. Close your program

What would you do? Are there other solutions?

Legal Restrictions

Can you treat parents in your program differently with regard to the rates they pay? In general, yes, as long as the different rate structure does not discriminate against a federal- or state-protected class. Federal law does not include subsidized families as a protected class; therefore, you could raise the rate for some or all of the subsidized families, or terminate some or all of these families. Check to see if your state law bans discrimination based on those receiving government subsidies.

Early Childhood Regulation Restrictions

Because you entered into a contract with your state subsidy program, you must follow state rules, if any, about rates. State rules will likely prohibit you from charging subsidized families a rate higher than the rate you charge private-pay families. States may or may not allow you to charge such families a copayment to bridge the gap between your private rate and subsidized payment. It's always appropriate to talk with your local subsidy worker before making changes in your payment terms with subsidized families.

Ethical Standards

The NAEYC Code of Ethics Supplement says, "We shall apply all policies regarding obligations to families consistently and fairly." Does this mean if you raise your rates for one family you must raise the rates for all? What about terminating all families rather than just one? Sometimes being consistent would not be fair. Your program could raise rates or terminate families based on how long they have been enrolled in your program. Or, instead, you could decide to fill open spaces in your program only with private-pay families.

Your Decision

Making financial decisions can be difficult when they directly affect families in your care, particularly low-income families. In addition, you should also take into consideration how your decision will impact your staff. One of the NAEYC Supplement's ideals is to "secure adequate and equitable compensation" for your staff (I-3.4). In the end, you may end up spreading the financial burden among staff, subsidized families, and private-pay families.

MAKING YOUR CONTRACT AND POLICIES WORK FOR EVERYONE

Your program's contract states that pickup time is 6:00 p.m. Worried about being short-staffed, you tell a prospective client, Sara Thompson, who contacts you about enrolling her child, that her pickup time will have to be 5:30 p.m. Sarah objects, saying she knows for a fact that other parents pick up by 6:00 p.m. "Why are you playing favorites?" she asks. What should you say and do?

There are no legal issues here because you are free to establish your own policies and we are assuming that Sara is not in a protected class. Whenever you change your contract with one family, you should assume that all families will hear about it. Trying to keep secrets won't work and is not respectful.

You can explain to Sara why her pickup time is different and say that you are willing to ask if there is another parent in your program who wants to exchange pickup times. Sara is not satisfied and says, "I'm going to complain to licensing that you are discriminating against me unless you allow me to pick up at 6:00 p.m." You can tell Sara that this is not an issue that licensing will act on, but offer to give her your licensor's phone number. If Sara continues to argue with you, let her know that you won't change her pickup time and ask her to tell you if she plans on enrolling her child on these terms. It's usually not productive to continue to justify your position. Sara may not be able to pick up any earlier and your reasons won't change this fact.

As we have noted, the primary purpose of a child care program's contract and policies is to facilitate communication with families. The better communication your program has with parents, the less likely you will have problems and conflicts. Thankfully, most child care programs don't take an overly legalistic stance with parents about their contract. Although programs could terminate parents immediately for any minor violation of the contract, few do so. You are part of a caring profession whose ethical standards call upon you to treat families with respect.

Here are some additional ideas to help make your contract and policies work better for you and the families in your program.

Making Changes in Your Contract and Policies

Because your program created the original contract and policies, you are free to make changes in them. Any change to a written contract must be in writing and signed by both parties. If not, the change is not enforceable. Let's say your contract states that the parent fee is $200 a week. In March you tell the parents you are going to raise their rates to $250 a week, and parents start paying you the higher amount. Your verbal agreement is not put in writing. In August one parent leaves without giving any notice, and owes you for two weeks under your contract. What does the parent owe you? Because the change to your contract was not put in writing, the parent owes $400 (not $500).

Therefore, whenever you seek to make a change in your contract, follow one of these steps:

1. Strike out the old language you wish deleted and write in by hand the new language. You and the parent should each put your initials and date next to the change.
2. Write out an addendum (amendment) to the contract on a separate piece of paper. Refer to the page in the contract that

the addendum is replacing (or adding). You and the parent should each sign and date the addendum.

3. Make the change in the contract and print out the entire contract. Have the parent sign it.

In all cases, give a copy of the change to the parent and keep the original for your records.

Reviewing and Evaluating Your Contract and Policies

It's always a good idea to ask parents to give feedback about how well your program is meeting their needs. You can do this through normal daily conversations ("How are things going for you?" "Do you have any concerns about your child's care?"). You can also ask parents to fill out a written evaluation. Oftentimes, child care programs give written evaluations only when a parent is leaving. We recommend doing annual evaluations. Being able to identify concerns early on allows you time to respond to them before a parent leaves.

Some parents are more comfortable giving you verbal feedback, while others prefer communicating in writing. By giving parents both opportunities, you are more likely to get useful information. If the parents sign their evaluation forms, keep a copy in their files. Positive evaluations can be used later to help defend your program against a parental complaint or lawsuit.

You may also want to establish a policy that encourages parents to bring forward complaints they might have about the care of their child. Doing so can prevent small problems from becoming bigger. Your policy could inform parents to bring up concerns first with the head teacher and then with the director if their concerns are not addressed to their satisfaction. You should also give parents the number of your licensor to call. In addition, you want a staff policy that describes procedures to follow when parents make complaints. Basically, you want complaints addressed as soon as possible and all serious complaints communicated immediately to the director. Of course, staff should be trained to strictly follow all mandated reporting requirements.

Enforcing Your Contract and Policies

To effectively enforce your contract and policies, your program must take the first step and make sure you are complying with your own rules. Let's say your contract requires parents to pay for 10 paid holidays a year (including Thanksgiving and Christmas), but you aren't collecting for Thanksgiving. In this case it will be more difficult to enforce your rule requiring parents to pay for Christmas, since you aren't consistently following your contract.

To enforce your contract, it must state the consequences of a failure to follow its terms. The consequence can be money (e.g., a late-pickup fee), or you could end the agreement. The language of consequences should be specific: "Parents must pay a $10 a day late-payment fee. Failure to pay this fee after three days will result in a termination of the contract." Vague and incomplete language ("Parents will be assessed a late-payment fee.") hinders parents' ability to understand their responsibility and will make it more difficult for you to enforce.

When a parent violates the contract or policies, most child care centers will talk it out and resolve the problem quickly. You are free to negotiate a solution: "Since apparently it is difficult for you to bring an extra change of clothes for your child each day, I propose that our center buy some clothes for your child and add the cost to your next bill." In the end, a repeated failure by a parent to follow any of your contract or policy terms should ultimately result in you ending your parent agreement. If you are not willing to terminate a parent for repeatedly violating a rule, you should eliminate your rule. It has become a voluntary suggestion, not a rule. If you haven't been consistently enforcing your rules in the past, it's never too late to start doing so now.

Ending Your Contract

Let's say you have tried unsuccessfully to work out a conflict with a parent and have decided to terminate your agreement. How do you go about doing this to reduce the risk of a lawsuit? The most important thing to do is to follow the terms of your contract. If your contract requires you to give a 2-week written notice, do so.

Your termination notice should be brief: "We are terminating care under the terms of our contract. The last day of care for _____ (name of child) will be on _____ (date)."

Do not give any written explanation for the termination. Doing so could upset the parents and make it more likely that they will make a complaint about your program. A written explanation may also lead the parents to believe that you discriminated against them illegally. For example, you give a parent a notice that says "We cannot continue to provide care for your child because of your failure to attend parent conferences." If the parent couldn't attend any of the meetings because she had a Bible study class at her Catholic church, she may believe you are discriminating against her because of her religion.

There are circumstances where you will want flexibility to terminate a contract without giving notice:

- A parent deliberately violates your contract or policies.
- A parent falsely accuses your staff of child abuse or neglect.
- A parent physically threatens staff members.
- A parent owes money and refuses to follow a separate payment agreement.
- A parent spreads false rumors about your program to others.

In these situations your program faces immediate damage in the form of loss of income, loss of reputation, or a lawsuit. You want to be able to reduce the possibility of further damage by ending your agreement immediately. Therefore, we recommend that you put in your contract, "The ABC Child Care Center may terminate this contract at will." Don't list reasons for when you will do so, because you will never be able to anticipate all future problems. It is not illegal or unethical to require parents to give a 2-week notice while giving your program the right to terminate immediately. You must be able to protect your program in the above circumstances. Before adopting this termination rule, talk to your licensor about whether this would be in violation of any state rules.

If your contract requires giving parents a 2-week termination notice and you fail to do so, a parent could argue that you broke the contract. If this does happen, you can defend yourself by saying that the parent's behavior threatened the safety of others or was creating a significant harm to your program.

A parent who leaves without giving the proper notice will be able to defend her violation of the contract in court if she can show that your program was violating the contract by mistreating her child or providing inadequate care.

Going to Court to Enforce Your Contract

The vast majority of conflicts between a child care center and parents are resolved quickly and do not lead to a lawsuit. When child care centers do sue parents, it's almost always for money owed under their contract. The best way to avoid the situation of a parent leaving owing you money is to require parents to pay you at least a week in advance and pay for the last 2 weeks of care at the time of enrollment. By adopting these two rules, parents will never be able to leave owing your center money.

We don't recommend using credit-reporting agencies (e.g., ProviderWatch) to weed out prospective clients who have a bad payment history. Requiring parents to pay in advance negates the need for such services. We also don't recommend that you share the names of parents who left owing money with other centers. This is a violation of confidentiality (see Chapter 7) and it can lead to an accusation against your center for defamation. Let's say you tell center #2 that Patricia Owens owes you money. Patricia later pays what she owes you. But, when center #2 (which doesn't know Patricia has paid you) tells center #3 that Patricia hasn't paid her bills, center #2 is guilty of defamation for sharing false information about Patricia that damages her reputation.

If parents do owe your center money, we strongly urge you to do everything possible to avoid taking parents to court. Some child care centers decide not to go to court, partly because the parents are low-income (making collecting money difficult) and partly because they may be afraid of harming their reputation as an organization that cares about families.

It is your decision about how to handle unpaid bills, but centers that don't set up systems to ensure being paid put their programs at risk financially. You can always compromise and negotiate a solution, but unless a parent is destitute with little hope of being able to pay, we believe that child care centers should use the court system as a last resort.

Before going to court, you may want to consider using a mediation service in your area (see Chapter 2). Neither party is obligated to follow the mediator's recommendations, and you still have the option of going to court. If the parent refuses to use the mediation process, bring this fact up later in court. It will increase your credibility as someone acting in good faith.

Before making the decision to go to court, send the parent a "demand letter." A demand letter spells out what you want the parent to do and what will happen if he or she doesn't comply. It should contain the following:

1. The amount the parent owes you under the contract
2. A demand for payment by a specific deadline
3. A notice that you will take legal action if the parent doesn't respond by the deadline

A demand letter shows you are serious about collecting money owed. Sometimes parents will pay after receiving the letter. You can make a decision later about whether to take the parents to court or not.

Some child care programs use collection agencies to collect unpaid bills. These agencies will contact parents and put pressure on them to pay you. Look under "Collection Agencies" online or in the Yellow Pages. The advantage of using such services is that you don't have to spend any more staff time pursuing the parent. The disadvantage is that the collection agency will take a portion of unpaid fees it collects.

To file a legal complaint against a parent, go to the small claims court in the courthouse in the county where the parent lives. After you fill out a short form and pay a small filing fee (usually less than $100), you and the parent will receive a notice in the mail telling both parties to appear in court for a hearing. It's not necessary to hire a lawyer to take a parent to small claims court. The amounts of money are usually too small to make it cost effective to hire one, and it's relatively easy for your staff to handle it.

At the hearing, bring your contract and state your case clearly: The parent violated the contract and your program suffered financially as a result. Records of your attempts to negotiate, requests for mediation, and a copy of your demand letter will support your position. In general, you will win cases in which you provided child care for which the parent didn't pay you. You should also win cases where the parent leaves without giving the proper notice.

Oftentimes parents will defend their nonpayment by making complaints about the care your program provided. Your best defense against this is to raise these points:

1. The parent never complained before he or she owed you money.
2. The parent never complained to licensing.
3. The parent's complaints to licensing were unfounded.

By following the guidelines in this chapter, you should be able to reduce conflicts with parents and resolve most issues without having to resort to legal actions.

4 Building Partnerships with Families

Preventing Sticky Situations and Promoting Clear Expectations

Children are the heart of our work; however, parents are our primary customers. Without a child's family, we can accomplish little, especially if our program is tuition-dependent. By setting clear, written expectations with parents at enrollment, we prevent costly misunderstandings later.

Save yourself from being blindsided. From the start with families, clarify and agree in writing on shared expectations. In advance, establish policies and procedures to defuse problems before they arise. Your preventative actions will give you and parents peace of mind.

By setting and maintaining policies and procedures with families, you:

1. prevent issues if teachers babysit for program families;
2. develop a "hold harmless" policy if staff babysit for families;
3. establish who has the right to pick up a child at the end of the day;
4. avoid being caught in the middle between parents in custody disputes;
5. assist parents with joint custody in developing a workable contract for who will pick up the child and when;
6. inform parents of how you will keep their child safe if an authorized person does not appear to be able to safely transport the child;
7. prevent children from leaving the program in vehicles that do not meet safety standards;
8. avoid liability from buckling a child into a safety seat or seatbelt;
9. prevent underage persons from being on the authorized list for picking up children;
10. practice how to address crisis situations, such as an intoxicated parent demanding to pick up her child.

Maintaining cordial and authentic relationships with family members is our hallmark. However, issues arise daily—both predictable and unexpected—that can damage our relationships with children's families. In this chapter, we'll look at ways to prevent sticky conflicts and how to effectively address complications when they arise.

Let's consider these issues one at a time. By this chapter's end, you will have many tools in your toolkit to ensure parental contentment and confidence in your program. You will also feel better prepared and more confident thanks to these policies, procedures, and practices.

WHEN TEACHERS BABYSIT FOR PROGRAM FAMILIES

Case Study: Pros and Cons of Babysitting

Preschool lead teacher Ramona is a favorite with most families. The Barry family, for example, hires Ramona every weekend to babysit their twins, Zackary and Zena. Ramona is like a second mother to the twins and a family member to the parents. Ramona is even included on family vacations at the beach. Ramona hears a rumor that you will no longer allow staff babysitting for families. She needs the income, loves the children like her own, and has settled into a routine.

Early childhood teachers like Ramona often work at multiple jobs to survive financially. Over the years, teachers have grown accustomed to working as babysitters for program families. After all, parents and children know and trust their teachers. Teachers love the children and need the work. Babysitting seems like a win-win arrangement.

But is it? Consider these possibilities. While babysitting, teacher Ramona trips and injures one of the twins. The stricken parents sue the program, exclaiming, "We only hired her because she works for you!"

A second possible issue with staff babysitting is favoritism. Luxuriating in one-on-one attention from a babysitting teacher in their homes, children can demand the same special treatment in the classroom. "My teacher likes me best. She even comes to my house," boasts preschooler Zackary. Confidentiality may also become an issue. The Barry family asks teacher Ramona to join them on a ski weekend. Other families or teachers may feel resentful. Or, Ramona finds herself hearing more than she wants to know about the family's private lives. Mrs. Barry confides in Ramona about her battle with prescription drug addiction. Professional boundaries blur. As a mandated reporter of suspected neglect or abuse, Ramona feels conflicted.

A seemingly simple win-win arrangement, like babysitting for program families, can cause unwanted headaches and possible legal problems. Given these potential issues, what would you say to teacher Ramona?

Which response below is the best course of action for Director Nia?

Quiz

Baby Rafiq's parents ask infant teacher Winette to babysit for Rafiq on Friday nights. Rafiq's parents trust Winette and value the strong and caring bond she has built with Rafiq. The parents look forward to their Friday "date night" thanks to Winette's babysitting. When Winette tells the director, Nia, about her new job, Nia responds:

1. Great. You'll do a fine job.
2. You should post a notice on the parent bulletin board announcing your babysitting services.
3. Our policy forbids babysitting by staff for families in our program.
4. Our policy forbids babysitting for program families. However, if Rafiq's parents sign a "hold harmless" document, you may be able to take the job.

Nia's safest response is either: (3) Our policy forbids babysitting for program families; or, (4) Our policy forbids babysitting unless parents sign a "hold harmless" document. If Rafiq's parents insist on hiring Winette, they, Winette, and Nia will have to agree in writing for Winette to continue babysitting.

Can We Allow Staff to Babysit Without Being Liable?

Programs that allow staff to babysit for families can be sued if the child is harmed. Logically, you might ask, "Isn't this just between the babysitter and the family?" You may believe the risk lies solely with the family. They hire their own babysitters. The family is under no obligation to hire your teachers as babysitters.

The answer is: Programs *can* be liable if a child is harmed while a staff member is babysitting. Why is this? First, the family met the teacher through the program and relied upon the program's representation that the teacher is qualified to work with children. Second, the teacher is *in an employment relationship with you*. Your hiring of him or her carries both the expectation and representation of your teacher's professional, "do-no-harm" behavior.

When parents hire teachers to babysit, they do so based in part because you hired the teacher to work at your program. Because the teacher

is currently employed by the program, parents assume that only qualified teachers are hired. Families trust and rely upon the program leader's judgment about who is a qualified early childhood professional.
Like it or not, your program can be held accountable.

"NO BABYSITTING" POLICY

Staff members cannot babysit for families whose children are enrolled in our
program.

Here's how colleague Ron McGuckin (n.d.) explains program
liability for teachers who babysit:

> A program may be held liable for the actions of an employee while the
> employee is caring for clients' children because there is a "causal connec-
> tion" between the program and the employee that creates an "implied
> reference" as to the competence of the employee. The causal connection
> implied that if the employee was not employed by the program, then the
> employee would not have been hired by the client to babysit. Because
> the client relied on the judgment of the program in hiring the employee,
> the program may be included in a lawsuit if something happens to a
> child.

As a result, programs need to consider a "no babysitting" policy
for both staff and family handbooks.

The "Hold Harmless" Option

Colleagues at a number of national for-profit programs offer an
option to parents, like the Barrys and Rafiq's parents, who insist on
hiring teachers as babysitters. Parents can choose to essentially waive
their right to hold the program liable should a child be harmed while a
teacher babysits.

In that case, parents agree to *hold* your program *harmless*. Parents
who sign a *hold harmless* agreement and hire a teacher to babysit
acknowledge that they:

1. are aware of the program's "no babysitting" policy; and,
2. accept the consequences of their choice in choosing to bypass
   the policy.

These parents would complete, sign, and date a "Consent to Hold Program Harmless for Staff Babysitting" form such as the sample one provided.

CONSENT TO HOLD _____ (PROGRAM'S NAME) HARMLESS FOR STAFF BABYSITTING

We/I _____ parents/legal guardians of _____ (name of child/ren) agree to hold _____ (Name of program) harmless for any injury that our child may experience while teacher _____ (teacher's name) babysits for our child/ren _____ (child/ren's names) on _____ (fill in the date). We are aware of the program's No Babysitting Policy, and choose to take exception to that policy.

Signatures required below:

Parent/Legal Guardian _____ Date _____
Director _____ Date _____
Teacher _____ Date _____

How frequently do these "hold harmless" forms need to be completed and signed by parents? Some programs require parents to sign and date a new copy of this form each time they hire a staff member to babysit.

Other programs require parents to complete the form periodically, for example, once at the beginning of each semester or school year. In either case, the completed form must be kept on file with a copy given to the family.

THINK ABOUT IT

Given these options, do you think your program would benefit from adding a "no babysitting" policy? Would you include the "hold harmless" option for parents? How frequently would you require all parties to sign the form?

Programs, like individuals, can be sued for many reasons. Having a "no babysitting" policy and "hold harmless" documentation will not stop your program from being sued. However, if you make sure the "no babysitting" policy and "hold harmless" forms are publicized, completed, and kept up to date, you render your program less likely to be liable.

> **THINK ABOUT IT**
>
> Rafiq's parents sign a "hold harmless" form each time they hire Winette to babysit for Rafiq. Winette leaves your program to teach at a nearby program. She continues to babysit for Rafiq. If Winette causes injury to Rafiq, can your program be sued?

AUTHORIZED LISTS FOR PICKUP

Case Study: Documenting Custody Rights

Solange enrolled her two daughters, Maria (3½) and Gladys (2) over a year ago at your program. You cannot find any documents indicating who has custody of the girls. Solange's brother and sister, included on her Authorized List to pick up the girls, have never come to the center.

Solange asks to meet with you in private. She breaks down sobbing and tells you of her narrow escape from the girls' abusive father, Wallace, back in Arkansas. Just then, Wallace, a clean-cut businessman, knocks on your door, asking for his children whom, he says, Solange kidnapped from him.

Preventing Problems

We often assume the person who enrolls the children has legal custody of those children. Enrolling parents or legal guardians sign contracts and are responsible for paying the fees. They identify whom to contact in an emergency if they are not available. They also prepare the Authorized List naming who can pick up the children in their stead.

Do you see potential problems with this assumption that the enrolling parent has legal custody? Without documentation, we cannot for certain know if the person enrolling the children has legal right to that child.

> **THINK ABOUT IT**
>
> Take a look at Solange's case. What would you do? What could you have done at enrollment to prevent this situation?

Assumptions were made at enrollment that Solange is the mother and has custody of Maria and Gladys. No legal documents supporting that assumption were filed.

Only later does Solange claim the children's father, Wallace, is an abuser from whom she fled. Wallace claims Solange kidnapped his daughters. Now we have a brush fire that can scorch the children, parents, and your program. The legal and psychological ramifications of not clarifying custody at enrollment could singe everyone.

Documenting Legal Rights When Children Are Enrolled

Let's look at what we can do in advance to prevent custody conflicts from arising. Consider requiring individuals who enroll a child to provide documentation of their legal right to the child. This step may seem unnecessary if families are well known to you. Especially in small communities where everyone knows everyone, can't we assume the enrolling family member has legal custody?

You will have to choose whether to be safe or sorry. What if you require documentation of custody from only one or two enrolling families? Those families may feel singled out or less trusted by you. To be fair, if you require documentation from one family, require it from everyone.

Documentation may be in the form of the children's birth certificates accompanied by the parents' identification. Judgments of adoption and guardianship, along with foster parent documentation, will also suffice (Child Care Law Center, 2005). Keep this documentation in the child's file. Update the information if the parent's legal status changes. Taking this step at enrollment prevents future trouble.

When a Parent Does Not Want to Reveal Information About the Other Parent

Not every enrolling parent is willing to acknowledge or list the other parent. Some parents may be offended or hurt when you require information about the child's other parent. Some mothers, for example, may be uncertain of the identity of the child's father. Other parents may withhold information for financial reasons. Still others may fear the dire consequences of being discovered as illegal immigrants (National Association for the Education of Homeless Children and Youth, 2010).

Explain to any enrolling parent why your program needs this information. Show them the policy in your family handbook.

BOTH PARENTS' RIGHT TO PICK UP THE CHILD

Under the laws of the state of _____, both parents may have the right to pick up their child unless a court document restricts that right. The enrolling parent who chooses not to include the other parent's name on the authorized list for pickup must file an official court document such as the following:

- Current restraining order
- Sole-custody decree
- Divorce decree stating sole custody
- Judgment of adoption
- Foster parent documentation

Absent this documentation, the program may release the child to either parent, provided that parent documents biological or adoptive parenthood of that child. The parent must provide the program with updated legal documents when any changes occur.

Consider again the case study about Solange and Wallace. If Solange had produced either her sole-custody decree of her children or a current restraining order against Wallace, she could have freed herself from living in fear that Wallace could take his daughters. When Wallace arrived, the program director could have told him why the children could not be released to him. In cases like this, you may also need to call for police assistance if you fear the children, teachers, or yourself are in danger.

If Wallace claims he can provide documentation that he has custody of Maria and Gladys, he will need to do so (Child Care Law Center, 2005). You, however, do not have to act as an officer of the court nor do you need to take action on the spot. Ask for help. Contact your attorney, local police, licensor, or court administrators to validate Wallace's claim.

Show Wallace your policy, Both Parents' Right to Pick Up the Child. Identify how he can document his right to the girls. Explain that you have not met him before and are not comfortable releasing the children until you know for sure he is their parent who has a legal right to take the children.

Move as quickly and expeditiously as you can to get the required documentation. Use your emotional intelligence to respect his feelings of urgency. Back yourself up with other professionals who can step in and defuse the situation. Above all, make sure that Maria and Gladys are not exposed to the conflict. Keep them engaged in a safe and supportive place while you are handling things in your office.

Documentation of Immigrant Families

In the case of immigrant parents, issues can escalate rapidly. Parents without citizenship, who are under threat of deportation as "illegal aliens," may be terrified to provide you with documentation. State laws are changing rapidly about the rights or lack thereof of immigrants (Serrie, 2011). Check with your licensor and/or attorney to find out your legal obligations.

You may also want to hear author Eileen Kugler's advice on how to partner with immigrant families. She suggests many ways we can be sensitive to each family's needs while paying attention to changing legal mandates. To hear her ideas, go to: http://www.bamradionetwork.com/index.php?option=com_content&view=article&id=547:jackstreet54&catid=69:infobamradionetworkcom&Itemid=144.

The "Do-No-Harm" Standard

What if Solange kidnapped the girls from Wallace and made up the story about Wallace being an abuser? This type of desperate situation would put everyone at risk, especially the vulnerable girls! Call the police immediately to report a possible felony. NAEYC's core value in the Code of Ethical Conduct and Statement of Commitment (2005, p. 3) is "Above all, we shall not harm children."

To prevent drama and danger like this, take these steps when enrolling children:

- Require each parent to provide documentation of custody.
- Discuss your policy, Both Parents' Right to Pick Up the Child, with the enrolling parent.
- If the enrolling parent chooses not to list the other parent on the Authorized List, advise the parent that appropriate documentation of her or his sole right to the child must be filed with you.
- If the enrolling parent does not provide that documentation, inform her or him that the other parent may have a right to pick up the child.

Should drama or danger escalate, take the steps in the section "Safe-Departure Policy" immediately (appears toward the end of the chapter).

Shared-Custody Agreements Prevent Release-Time Drama

Sometimes we feel we are in the midst of a soap opera. Parents like Solange and Wallace, who cannot stand each other, make up and get back together. Solange confesses Wallace was not abusive; she was just upset when she said that. Wallace forgives Solange for deserting him and taking the girls. Back together and sharing custody, they seem like a happy family. Maria and Gladys thrive.

Later, like the tides, the relationship again ebbs. Solange has met a "better man" named Thomas. Wallace has found his life partner in Chauncey. Solange refuses to let Chauncey pick up the children. Wallace demands that Thomas be kept off the Authorized List. Now who has the right to create the Authorized List for pickup?

In fact, each parent with physical custody of the children can create an Authorized List (Child Care Law Center, 2005). To keep arrangements clear, invite the parents to sit down together, with a facilitator if necessary, to complete the following agreement:

SHARED-CUSTODY AGREEMENT FOR RELEASE-TIME PICKUP OF CHILDREN

We, _____ and _____, parents/legal custodians of _____, agree that _____ (Parent #1) will pick up _____ondays through Wednesdays; _____ (Parent #2) will pick up _____ on Thursdays and Fridays.

If a parent attempts to pick up the children on the other parent's day, that parent must document the consent of the other parent to the change in schedule.

Should continuous changes occur, both parents will sign and file a revised agreement with the program promptly. If parents cannot continue to carry out this agreement over time, they may be asked to find another center.

Each parent will create and maintain his or her authorized list for the days on which that parent has agreed to pick up the child.

This Shared-Custody Agreement for Release-Time Pickup of Children schedule, when completed by both parents together, prevents flare-ups. Solange can decide who is on her Authorized List and keep Chauncey off her list. Wallace can put Chauncey on his list, while not naming Thomas. Each parent creates and maintains decision making for who can act in his or her stead in picking up the children.

Custody Rights of Stepparents

What happens if either or both Solange and Wallace remarry or marry another person for the first time? What custody rights do their new partners/spouses have to Maria and Gladys?

> A stepparent does not have legal rights to his or her spouse's child unless the stepparent legally adopts that child.

Courts consider a stepparent's relationship with a child to be a "social relationship." A social relationship like this carries no custody rights: "A stepparent is not entitled to, and has no legal right to, custody and/or visitation absent a court order. The stepparent can only be authorized by his or her spouse, the child's parent of legal and physical custody, to have 'custody' of the child at a particular time" (Child Care Law Center, 2005, p. 24). Even if Thomas acts as if he is the girls' father, he has no legal custody rights unless he legally adopts the children. The same is true for Chauncey.

Concerns for the Child's Safety at Release-Time

Parents who have physical custody of a child have the right to pick up their child. Technically, if someone at the program refuses to release the child to the parent, that person can be sued for kidnapping the child.

What can you do if you fear for the child's safety or well-being if the parent takes the child? Consider preschooler Cole's case study.

INSTITUTING A SAFE-DEPARTURE POLICY

Case Study: Safety Concerns at Release Time

Cole, almost 4, was a bright, talkative, and playful child when he entered your program 2 years ago. Since that time, Cole's parents, William Wilkins and Nora Epstein, have separated and are slogging their way through a long, mud-slinging custody battle for Cole.

William tells you his wife "has a drinking problem." Nora complains her husband's revolving door of new "mothers" is upsetting Cole. Cole, now quiet and cautious, asks his teacher, Sarah, if she will be his mom. You and your staff attempt to stay neutral and respectful to both parents. Your concern for Cole's well-being grows each day.

Just before the December holidays, Cole's mother, Nora, careens into the program bellowing "Ho! Ho! Ho!" to everyone. She stumbles into the classroom, grabs Cole, and insists she's driving him to the ice cream shop. Teacher Sarah thinks she smells alcohol on Nora's breath. Nora is belligerent and refuses to lower her voice. Cole hides behind his teacher. Nora yells, "What are you gonna do? Sue me! Come on, Cole, let's get out of this dump."

Regardless of her attitude or condition, Mom Nora has custody of her son. Technically she has the right to take him with her. You, however, fear if you release Cole to his Mom, both Cole and his Mom may end up in a crash on the side of the road.

How could you have prevented this wrenching dilemma? Imagine if you had shared and discussed a "Safe-Departure Policy" with Cole's parents at enrollment. Here's an example of what a written notice might look like:

SAFE-DEPARTURE POLICY NOTICE

If we are concerned for the safety or well-being of your child should we release that child to you, we will inform you of our concern and call another person on your Authorized List to pick up the child.

If we are concerned for your child's safety when a person on your Authorized List picks up your child, we will phone you immediately and/or call another person on your Authorized List to pick up your child.

If both parents agree to this policy, they consent to your taking steps to ensure their child's safety (Child Care Law Center, 2005, pp. 12–13). You can show Nora the policy and her signature, call William or another authorized person, offer Nora a cup of coffee and engage her in conversation, all while preparing for another person to safely pick up Cole.

In crisis times like this, having built candid and trusting relationships with each parent and family member pays dividends. Learn and use the name of each parent, even if you are "not good with names." Personal connections will help carry you and parents through difficult times like this. You will feel more able to directly tell Nora why you are concerned for Cole's safety if he departs with her.

What to Say to a Parent Who May Be Under the Influence

Would you tell Nora you fear she has been drinking? After all, she is not being herself, and her loud and belligerent behavior is out of character. Most of us are not medical professionals. We don't keep a breathalyzer handy to assess whether someone has been drinking.

If we accuse Nora of being drunk (especially within earshot of others), we can potentially be sued for slander. Slander is a verbal statement that harms another person's reputation in the community.

Keep in mind other possible causes of Nora's behavior. She may be taking medication that causes unstable gait, slurred articulation, or other off-balance behavior. She may have a medical condition, such as vertigo, that causes her to stagger and fall. The better you know each parent, starting at enrollment, the better equipped you are to deal with crises.

Show Nora her initials on the Safe-Departure Policy. Let her know you and she both have Cole's best interests at heart. However, avoid accusing her of being intoxicated. If she tells you she has been drinking, she opens the door. You can now talk with her about Cole's lack of safety if he is in a vehicle with an adult who is under the influence.

Ensuring Use of Safety Seats and Seatbelts

Your state statutes set standards for children's weight and/or size requirements for car safety seats.

> All 50 states require child safety seats for infants and children from birth. Children may move up to an adult safety belt between the ages of 4 and 9, depending upon the state. Additionally, many states consider a child's weight and height when establishing requirements. For example, Tennessee requires children under the age of 1 or under 20 pounds to be in a rear-facing infant seat. Children between the ages of 1 and 3, and over 20 pounds, may be in a forward-facing infant seat. Children between the ages of 4 and 8, and less than 4'9" tall, must be in a booster seat. Children under the age of 9 and under 4'9" must be in a rear seat if available, and rear-seat riding is suggested for children ages 9 to 12. Tennessee's law is more detailed than those of some other states, but it exemplifies the requirements of many others. (Governors Highway Safety Association, 2012)

Not everyone complies with these laws. A director in Pennsylvania told me about a father who was so proud of his new truck's leather interior that he refused to install a car safety seat that might mar the leather.

Some people feel their First Amendment right to free expression of speech also allows them to choose whether to use safety seats, for example, or helmets for motorcycles. Iowa, Illinois, and New Hampshire do not have motorcycle helmet laws whatsoever. Other states either require riders under a certain age to wear helmets or require all riders to wear helmets (Insurance Institute for Highway Safety, 2012). Our job is to make sure children are safe when they leave our programs.

The director in Pennsylvania took a preventative approach. She offered families a quarterly safety inspection of car seats and seatbelts. She told families the local police department's "Officer Friendly" would be available to check car seats and seatbelts for safety. The officer also made sure parents knew how to safely buckle children into the seats. Inevitably, at least 20% of families in that program learned they needed to make changes.

The sample Vehicle Safety Seats and Seatbelts Policy shows a direct approach that puts all families on notice that you expect them to keep children safe.

VEHICLE SAFETY SEATS AND SEATBELTS POLICY

Adults who transport children in vehicles must maintain and use safety seats and seatbelts in compliance with state laws. Failure to follow these standards will result in our calling another person on the Authorized List to pick up the child. As mandated reporters, we also will report your not using a safety seat to the police and Department of Social Services.

Some police departments, hospitals, and other authorized organizations offer courses in how to install car safety seats and buckle children into the seats safely. Some hospitals even provide car safety seats to families of newborns at the hospital. Offer families information about the course and your local hospital's policy of providing car safety seats. For a list of police departments, hospitals, and other organizations that provide this service, go to the National Highway Traffic Safety Administration website (see Appendix: Helpful Websites).

If you or your employee either installs a car seat for a family or buckles the child into the seat and the seat malfunctions, you may be liable. Some directors designate a staff member to take the course (mentioned above) and be credentialed in the process. If that credentialed staff member assists families, she is likely to have less liability if the car seat or buckle malfunctions. The safest approach to avoid liability is to not get involved in installing car seats or buckling children into the seats. (See Appendix: Helpful Websites.)

Minimum Age Requirement for Authorized List

Check your state's regulations regarding who may be placed on the Authorized List. California, for example, has no specified age, whereas New York requires a person to be 18. You may find that parents in your state have discretion to list whomever they want to pick up their children. Parents are assumed to have the child's best interests in mind.

> ### THINK ABOUT IT
>
> Parents can get especially pressed for time at the end of the day. Consider the sample scenarios. What could you do to prevent problems like these from arising?

Here are some sample scenarios:

Scenario 1: Baby Tanya's dad, waiting in the car, sends Tanya's 11-year-old sister to gather up Tanya and her take-home items.

Scenario 2: A 13-year-old mom with custody of her baby boy wants to send her 12- and 13-year-old friends with a stroller to bring her baby home.

Scenario 3: Babysitter Amanda, a mature 14-year-old who has completed a babysitting course, cares for the Petrozullio's toddler children almost every Saturday evening. Mr. Petrozullio wants to place Amanda on the Authorized List. He asserts: "We absolutely trust Amanda to walk the children home safely. You're not questioning our parental prerogative, are you?"

Power struggles with parents are counterproductive. Of course, parents can—and do—determine who is qualified and able to care for their children. You, however, can institute and uphold a high standard for safety at your program. Consider adding an "Age Requirement for Being on an Authorized List" policy to your parent handbook. This policy alerts all families that adults are expected to accompany children home safely.

> ### AGE REQUIREMENT FOR BEING
> ### ON AN AUTHORIZED LIST
>
> Persons on the Authorized List must be at least 18 years of age and able to document their age and identity.

Remember, state licensing standards set the minimum requirement for your program's compliance. You can institute a higher standard. Courts tend to support policies that set a higher standard for quality. Seeking accreditation also indicates your intention to go beyond what state licensing regulations require.

Damage Control Versus Calling in the Authorities

We aim to prevent as many mishaps from occurring as we can. By instituting the policies in this chapter, you will go a long way toward preventing power struggles and potentially dangerous moments. Sometimes, however, troubles still occur.

Perhaps a parent like Nora, who appears to be intoxicated, will stomp out of your program regardless of what you say and do. Nora and William might spark a screaming match in the lobby of your program. Our task is to "Above all, do no harm" to children. Programs need a damage-control procedure to stop or minimize the harm of an explosive situation.

THINK ABOUT IT

What has worked for you in defusing upset or out-of-control family members? At what point do you call in the authorities?

If a child, staff member, or you are in immediate danger, call 911. If you sense you have some leeway before a situation erupts, consider taking the intermediary steps outlined in the Release-Time Crisis Procedure. If the child is in danger, move directly to Step 6.

RELEASE-TIME CRISIS PROCEDURE

Before we release a child to a person whose behavior is potentially unsafe, we may take the following steps:

1. Remove the child from the immediate environment; comfort and reassure the child of his or her safety
2. Share our concern with the person
3. Remind the person of our Safe-Departure Policy
4. Enlist the help of an appropriate family member, either in person or by phone
5. Call another person on the Authorized List to step in and pick up the child
6. Call the police
7. Report potential abuse or neglect to appropriate authorities

What If No One Picks Up the Child?

Unexpected events overturn our best-laid plans. Imagine this scenario: Baby Rhina's mom is rushed to a hospital, unconscious after a car accident. Dad is overseas in a secret Marine combat operation and can't be reached. No one else on the Authorized List answers the phone. Your program has already closed and you are late for your son's Little League play-off game. What about Rhina?

If you haven't yet found yourself in a situation like this, you are likely to experience it. No one wants to imagine that a child will be left behind without family to care for her. We all hope that Rhina will not have to face this trauma. What is the right thing to do?

If we take Rhina to the Little League game or home with us, we face potential liability by failing to separate boundaries between work and home. What if Rhina is injured at the game or while riding in your personal car? You may be personally responsible.

"Good Samaritans" are not always rewarded for their efforts. In fact, Good Samaritans can be liable if harm comes to the person they are attempting to save.

The wisest approach to the left-behind-child dilemma is to discuss upfront with the parent what you will do if no one on the Authorized List, including the parents, can be contacted and the program is closing. Perhaps the parents will respond by adding other responsible people to their Authorized List. Perhaps they were unaware that even one lawsuit for taking a child home could financially shut down the whole center.

Take a look at the "If No One on the Authorized List Can Be Reached to Pick Up Your Child" policy. If you institute this policy, be sure you have a personal conversation with each enrolling family member so that expectations are clear before the problem develops.

IF NO ONE ON THE AUTHORIZED LIST CAN BE REACHED TO PICK UP YOUR CHILD

All attempts will be made in good faith to contact you and the others on your Authorized List.

If no one can be reached at the time the program closes, the Department of Social Services (DSS) along with the police department will be notified.

DSS will take custody of the child while further attempts to reach you are made.

INTRODUCING NEW POLICIES TO FAMILIES

If you decide to incorporate any of these policies, procedures, or practices into your program, use the due process approach (Chapter 1). Meet with appropriate groups to inform them of the change you want to make. Outline the benefits of making the change. Open the meeting to questions and comments. Give people ample time to reflect and offer their feedback.

Holding a "hearing" like this with parents will prepare them for revisions you make to the parent handbook. Hold similar discussions with your staff when a change affects them. Invite them to share their responses, including criticism of the proposed policy, with you. Incorporate their feedback, if advisable, into the actual handbook policy before you enact it. Due process helps people affected by change feel ownership of that change. Resistance is lessened.

Looking back at the many ways you can prevent or address end-of-day problems, what are you thinking might be most applicable and helpful to your program?

5 Keeping Your Child Care Center Safe for Everyone

Prevention Strategies

"Above all, we shall not harm children."

There is no disagreement about this fundamental point—the safety of children is the number one mission of your organization. It's the first principle of the NAEYC Code of Ethical Conduct and Statement of Commitment (P-1.1). It's also the first principle of the NAEYC Code of Ethical Conduct Supplement: "We shall place the welfare and safety of children above other obligations. . . ." (P-1.1)

In this chapter we discuss how to keep your child care center safe for the children, your staff, and the families you serve. We will pay particular attention to the preventative steps you can take to reduce the risk of accidents and ensuing lawsuits. We will also discuss how to handle child abuse allegations.

YOUR LEGAL DUTY

Keeping children safe is also your primary legal duty. Failure to fulfill this duty can result in fines, the loss of your center's license, and even jail time for you and your staff.

State child abuse laws and criminal statutes prohibit the maltreatment of children. The most extensive description of your responsibilities toward children can be found in your state's child care licensing rules, where safety issues dominate. Although the particulars of each state's rules vary, most of them cover the following:

- Rules that limit the number of children a staff person can care for
- Staff training requirements in first aid, cardiopulmonary resuscitation (CPR), and child abuse
- Policies to address emergencies, sick children, and behavior guidance
- Indoor and outdoor physical space requirements, water hazards, locks, fire extinguishers, smoke detectors, and so forth

- Transportation issues—child safety restraints, parent permission, and so forth
- Sanitation and health standards—pest control, hand washing, food safety, diapers, and so forth

If you are the administrator of a child care center, you are very familiar with these rules. Your primary job is to see that your staff follows them. There may be obstacles in your way: your board of directors is not fulfilling its oversight role, you have high staff turnover, or your state licensor has not inspected your program for many years because of state budget cutbacks. None of these obstacles, however, is an excuse for you to not meet your ethical and legal responsibilities to the children in your program.

As we discussed in Chapter 2, if your center is out of compliance with your state's licensing rules, you face a greater threat of a lawsuit and the likelihood of a higher damage award in a lawsuit.

Let's say that a toddler in your program falls from a swing set and injures her face. The teacher calls 911. Unfortunately, the child's face becomes infected and is permanently scarred. The doctor later says that the scar would have been much less noticeable if the teacher had applied first aid to slow the initial bleeding. The licensing investigation uncovers the fact that the toddler's teacher did not have the required first aid training.

The fact that your staff records have not been checked in the past 2 years is not going to prevent licensing from finding your center guilty of violating this licensing rule and imposing a sanction. The child's parents may use this rule violation as a reason to ask for more monetary damages against your center in their civil lawsuit.

Therefore, take all child care licensing rules seriously. They help protect children, your staff, and your center. Being in compliance is no guarantee that children won't be injured, but it can reduce the likelihood of allegations of staff negligence and decrease the damages awarded in a lawsuit.

Because child care rules can change, you want to be sure you are receiving notification of new rules. Find out how and where new rules are made public. As a backup, contact your state's licensing office at least once a year to make sure you have the most current information.

AN OUNCE OF PREVENTION

The risks of caring for a group of children are real: injuries, property damage, vehicle accidents, and lawsuits. Although you can never eliminate these risks, you can take a number of steps to reduce the risks to a manageable level.

Let's first look at a series of preventative steps you can take. Then we will describe how to handle special situations: caring for sick and injured children, keeping children safe on field trips, and child abuse.

After complying with your state's child care licensing rules, taking steps to prevent injuries is probably your best way to reduce risks. Never underestimate the power of commonsense precautions. In fact, failure to use common sense can lead to allegations of staff negligence. Here are some examples of the many preventative measures your program can follow:

- *Teacher walk-around*—Looking for safety hazards should be a never-ending task. Train your staff to regularly walk around the room they teach in and look for any potential hazards. Periodically, have a different teacher than the one normally in the classroom look for safety hazards through a fresh lens. The most common injury suffered by children in child care is falling down, so pick up or put away items on the floor. Closely examine things that children can climb to ensure that they will not be injured if they fall.
- *Sanitary standards*—The cleaner your program is, the lower your risk of illness for children and your staff. The most important practice to follow is hand washing on a regular basis. Following daily intra-day sanitizing and disinfecting processes for toys, diaper-changing areas, and table surfaces is an excellent way to reduce the spread of illness.
- *Third-hand smoke*—There is a risk to children and your staff from being exposed to smoke from parents, and even from children who live with parents who smoke. Child care centers may regulate smoking with stronger regulations than state and local laws. However, some laws/regulations require providers to inform parents of such stricter policies in a specific manner. For example, some policy guidelines may require you to clarify the purpose of the policy, develop a strategic enforcement and implementation plan, or educate parents and/or staff about the health risks.
- *Potluck suppers/food allergies*—Your program will be held responsible if a child becomes sick from the food served in your program. This includes food brought by parents to a potluck at your program. If children have food allergies, notify parents not to bring certain foods for the potluck (without identifying which children have allergies).

- *Communicable illnesses*—Every child care program should be guarding against the spread of communicable illnesses (flu, HIV, blood-borne pathogens, etc.). The NAEYC Code of Ethical Conduct requires centers to inform families if their child has been exposed to a communicable disease that might result in infection (P-2.9). State and county health agencies can offer resources. In Chapter 6 we will discuss how to comply with the Americans with Disabilities Act (ADA).
- *Emergency planning*—Preparedness includes creating plans for anticipated emergencies such as a fire, tornado, hurricane, earthquake, flood, or a violent parent. Do you have written procedures for how to handle each emergency?
- *Sudden Infant Death Syndrome (SIDS)*—Although the exact cause of SIDS is unknown, child care programs can reduce this risk by training staff to put babies to sleep on their backs, not confining them with blankets or other objects, and checking on them often. Years ago a child died of SIDS in a child care center in Minnesota. Because the program had good records showing how often staff checked on the baby, child care licensing took no negative action and the parents did not sue. In another case in Connecticut, the judge awarded $800,000 to the parents of a baby who died of SIDS in the home of a licensed family child care provider who saw the baby lying on her stomach and did nothing. Many states have laws relating to SIDS. In 11 states, child care center staff must have special training about SIDS: Arizona, California, Florida, Indiana, Minnesota, Nebraska, Tennessee, Texas, Washington, West Virginia, and Wisconsin. (For a detailed list of SIDS-related laws, see Appendix: Helpful Websites.)

CARING FOR SICK AND INJURED CHILDREN

Unfortunately, regardless of your prevention efforts, there is a good chance that children will become ill while in your child care program. When this happens, some parents may want you to care for their child while recovering from an illness or to treat their child's illness. Caring for children who are ill creates new risks that can be handled by establishing clear policies and procedures.

Your center is not obligated by any federal law to care for children who are sick. Therefore, your first policy in this area should cover under what conditions you will or will not accept children into your program who are sick. Your state child care licensing laws may set conditions under which you may not accept children who are ill (e.g., a child has a contagious illness). You may also be required to report certain illnesses to your state agency.

But, beyond these limitations, your center can set its own standards. Most centers will observe children when they arrive to detect signs of illness. You could refuse to accept children with a minor illness (e.g., a mild cold), or you could accept children suffering from most illnesses and provide special care for them.

If a child becomes sick while at your center, your responsibility is to see to it that the child receives appropriate medical care. This may mean giving medications to the child, providing a space for the child to lie down, calling the parent to pick up the child, or calling 911. Your first decision will be whether or not to allow the child to stay in your center. Whatever your decision, you want your actions to closely follow a written policy about how to handle these situations. You want your policy to spell out when you will refuse a child, how you will provide temporary care for a child who is ill, and under what circumstances you will call the parents or 911.

Giving Medications

Your state licensing rules will probably set out guidelines for when and how you can give medications to children in your center. This may include first getting parental permission by phone or in writing, as well as permission from the child's doctor. Because of the potential serious consequences of failing to properly issue medication, your policy should always be to get written parent and doctor permission, regardless of your state regulations. Put in writing the following information about each medication you are administering:

- Date medication was prescribed
- Name of the medication
- Dosage
- Time and dates medication is to be given
- Period of time over which the medication is to be given
- Prescribing physician's name and phone number
- Additional information about possible side effects, whether to give the medication with food, storage instructions (is refrigeration required?), and so on

You can get into legal trouble if you fail to follow parents' wishes or a doctor's orders. But, what if the doctor and one of the parents signs your medication permission form, but the other parent won't? Without the signature of the second parent, you should not administer the medication.

Nonprescription Medications

To be on the safe side, you should follow the same guidelines for nonprescription medications. Let's say a parent wants to leave a bottle of Tylenol with her child's teacher and is willing to sign a blanket medication authorization allowing the teacher to give it if the teacher thinks it's necessary. We don't recommend using such blanket authorizations. Any medication your staff is going to administer should be at the direction and authorization of the child's doctor.

Immunizations

Your state child care regulations likely require that children be immunized against illnesses such as measles, mumps, chickenpox, diphtheria, and whooping cough. Without such immunizations, your program could refuse to accept a child. A conflict can arise, however, when a parent refuses to allow her child to be immunized because of the parent's religious, medical, or philosophical beliefs. Some states allow parents to opt out for some of these reasons. All states and the District of Columbia allow medical exemptions. The District of Columbia and all states except Mississippi and West Virginia allow religious exemptions. Only 20 states allow philosophical exemptions: Arizona, Arkansas, California, Colorado, Idaho, Louisiana, Maine, Michigan, Minnesota, Missouri, New Mexico, North Dakota, Ohio, Oklahoma, Pennsylvania, Texas, Utah, Vermont, Washington, and Wisconsin.

Because of fears about the side effects of immunization, increasing numbers of parents are refusing to have their children immunized, especially for religious reasons. Some parents, who fear the possible side effects of a shot, may be raising a religious objection because that is the only way they can ensure their child does not get the shot. Although you can encourage parents to have their children immunized, do not try to challenge parents if you believe their objection is philosophical, rather than religious. Questioning parents' motives is likely to create more trouble. Talk with your licensing worker for help in resolving these disputes.

Injuries

It's almost impossible to prevent children from ever becoming injured in your center. Your state's child care licensing rules will spell out your responsibilities to treat injured children and contact parents. They will also indicate your responsibility to report injuries to the proper authorities. If your state doesn't already require it, keep careful records of all injuries. Contact your liability insurance agent immediately so the insurance company can conduct its own investigation. If the injury is minor and you aren't sure whether this should be reported to your insurance agent, contact your agent anyway. Let your agent give you guidance about when to report injuries to him or her. By contacting your insurance agent immediately, it will increase the chances that the matter can be settled quickly, without a lawsuit. This can help keep your insurance premiums stable and maintain the reputation of your center. (See Chapter 10 for more information about insurance.)

Biting

If there is a child who bites in your center, it is not appropriate to share this child's name with the parent of the child who was bitten. It can't help the situation. But it could make it more likely that one or both sets of parents will be unhappy and make complaints. Having a general policy of not sharing confidential information about children or their parents will go a long way to defusing this situation. (See Chapter 7 for details.)

Next, tell parents the steps you are taking to decrease the likelihood of the biting to reoccur. If parents are worried about the potential for biting to spread HIV, you should help parents understand that this is extremely unlikely. The blood of two children needs to be exchanged for the risk of HIV to increase. You may also advise parents of their rights to contact a bitten child's doctor. Although it is unlikely, bites can sometimes lead to infection. Your primary concern is the health and safety of the child, so suggesting medical attention should never be avoided because you are afraid you may be liable.

KEEPING CHILDREN SAFE WHEN OUTSIDE AND AWAY

Your program's responsibility to keep children safe continues when children are on a playground, field trip, or in a vehicle under your center's control.

Child care centers must check outside daily to make sure playground equipment and the area is in good shape. This may include picking up trash, raking mulch back into proper places, and so forth. A few state licensing agencies comply with Consumer Product Safety Commission rules on playground safety, which can be found in the CPSC Public Playground Safety Handbook (see References at the back of the book).

Your duty to keep children safe while on a field trip is the same as when the children are in your building. The risk of injury may be greater on a field trip because of the potentially unsafe environment at a park, children's museum, or other destination. The steps you can take to reduce risks include vigilant supervision by your staff, carrying first aid kits, obtaining signed permission forms from parents, and an emergency plan to deal with injuries that occur away from your building. You want to have a signed authorization form from parents to provide emergency medical treatment for their child when a parent cannot be reached immediately. This authorization form should also allow for emergency medical treatment when a child is on a field trip.

It's likely that your business liability insurance policy will cover your center for injuries suffered by children on field trips. Discuss with your insurance agent all possible circumstances when you will be supervising children away from your building to be sure your center is covered.

Field trip permission forms and emergency medical treatment forms are not a shield against a parent suing you if his or her child is injured. Liability waivers are also not a guarantee that you won't be sued. Following your state licensing rules regarding field trips, practicing commonsense safety standards, getting parental permission, and having adequate business liability insurance are your best safeguards against a lawsuit. See Chapter 10 for a discussion about insurance.

CHILD ABUSE

Perhaps the most important legal responsibility of a child care worker is to fulfill his or her duty as a mandated reporter of child abuse or neglect. We first discussed this in Chapter 2.

The NAEYC Code of Ethics directs child care programs to protect children by reporting suspected cases of child abuse or neglect to the appropriate authorities (P-1.9). The Code also directs child care workers to take "appropriate action in order to protect the child" when told of suspected child abuse or neglect by someone else (P-1.10). There is also an ethical duty to inform parents in these situations (P-1.11).

Your state child care licensing rules address how to respond to suspected cases of child abuse and neglect that you must follow. Failure to report suspected child abuse or neglect will result in severe penalties.

Therefore, you want to follow a three-step approach to help prevent child abuse or neglect:

1. Develop and implement policies that reduce the risks: careful supervision of children, staff background checks, and staff training on child development, sexuality, and positive guidance techniques (as well as cultural influences on these issues).
2. Document and keep records about child behavior, parent communication, and accidents and conflicts with parents or staff.
3. Educate your staff about child abuse and reporting laws to be sure they clearly understand their obligations as mandated reporters.

One practice some child care centers follow to be on the alert for signs of child abuse is to fill out a daily drop-off form for each child and ask parents to sign it. A staff person will examine the child for signs of physical bruises or marks and ask the parent a few questions about the child's medical condition. After the parent signs the form, the staff person puts it into the child's files.

What if your staff person, Maureen, does notice a bruise and the child's mother, Kay, admits hitting the child? Maureen should explain to Kay that she must follow your center's policy on reporting child maltreatment. Maureen may want to also consider asking Kay to join her in reporting the incident to child protection as a sign that she is open to receiving help.

Your center may also want parents to fill out a daily pickup form that states the condition of the child at pickup. This can help protect your staff against child abuse allegations. Let's say Nedra signs a pickup form that says her child, Tasha, had no marks on her. The next day, Nedra calls you to complain about a bruise on Tasha's right arm, claiming that her teacher caused the bruise by roughly grabbing the child during the previous day. You can use the signed pickup form as a defense.

Because each state has its own child abuse laws, they vary. Corporal punishment is permitted by parents in the home; however, some states and localities have enacted laws limiting or defining the practice. For example, excessive spanking or spanking children under a certain age may be illegal.

In 2008, the Minnesota Supreme Court ruled that spanking does not constitute abuse. The court found a man innocent who spanked his 12-year-old son 36 times with a paddle (Olson, 2008). On the other hand, if corporal punishment results in the death of a child, it is likely that parents will be found guilty of criminal laws. In 2006, a father was convicted of murder when the beating of his daughter with an electrical cable was called "torture" and led to the girl's death (Coen, 2006). Throughout the world, 29 countries have completely outlawed spanking in school or at home.

If you are ethically opposed to spanking, do not hesitate to forbid it in your center, even though it's not against state law. On the other hand, what should you do if Mrs. Jordan wants her child spanked even if state law prohibits it? Obviously, you cannot spank the child and you will probably have to discuss with Mrs. Jordan how you may be required to report her if you have a reasonable belief that she is spanking the child.

Child Abuse Investigations

Being accused of child maltreatment or abuse is everyone's worst nightmare. Let's look at how to handle an investigation by a child care licensor, a child protection worker, or the police.

Whenever a child is injured in your center, an outside agency will investigate your program. If you take a child to the hospital, medical professionals are required by law to notify child protection agencies if they suspect child abuse or neglect. Outside agencies may also ask the police to undertake their own investigation. The parents of the injured child may also call on these agencies or the police to get involved.

Accusations of child abuse and neglect can lead to the arrest of you or your employees and the shutting down of your center. You or your employees could be put in jail if found guilty in extreme cases. Because of the seriousness of these accusations, it's important for you to understand your legal rights at the beginning of any investigation. For purposes of our discussion, we will not make a distinction between whether your employee did or did not commit child abuse or neglect.

State Investigations. How you handle a licensing or child protection investigation may determine whether there will be a criminal investigation. Your state's child care rules probably require you to participate in the investigation. Your refusal to participate will likely cause your center to be shut down.

Therefore, you want to be prepared to be interviewed by your state child care agency. It's critical that you be truthful and consistent in your answers to questions from investigators. Do not assume, however, that if you are truthful, the persons asking you questions will believe you.

If your answers don't appear to make sense or are confusing or too inconsistent to be believable, it's extremely likely they will notify law enforcement authorities to conduct a criminal investigation. This is often how the police become involved in child care–related accidents.

Plan ahead by anticipating questions that may be asked of you and practice your answers. Here is a checklist of questions you should be prepared to answer:

- At what time and how did the accident happen?
- Where did the accident occur?
- Describe what happened to the child (nature of injuries, etc.).
- What time did you first learn about the incident?
- What did you or your staff do to help the child?
- What are the names of the people who were present when the incident happened?
- Did you notify the parent(s)? If so, when?
- Have you talked about this incident with anyone? Who (names, addresses, phone numbers)?
- What actions have you taken to make sure that a similar accident won't happen again?

Be consistent in your answers. This will be easier to do if you have kept clear documentation of all incidents in your program. Inconsistencies will be perceived as lies, even if you are not lying. Practice speaking your answers out loud to help you come across as confident and professional. Lying during an investigation carries its own criminal penalties (obstruction of justice). You could be jailed for lying even if you are found innocent of child abuse!

Whenever a child is injured in your center, notify all your employees that they should not talk to anyone about what happened other than to the proper authorities. This means not talking to other staff or to their spouses. If the investigator finds out that you or an employee told an inconsistent story to someone else, they may assume you are lying.

If there is any news media interest in the accusations of child neglect or abuse, designate one person among your staff to respond to all news media. Usually, this person will be the director (or your attorney). Anticipate what you will say if a reporter shows up at your center. Because of your confidentiality policy, you can tell reporters that you will not share any information about staff or families. You can say that you are cooperating with child care licensing or police investigations.

Criminal Investigations. If the police start asking questions of you or your staff, be aware of your rights. Most state child care licensing agencies require programs to cooperate with law enforcement investigations; however the Constitution provides individuals with protections, which do include the right to refuse to talk to officers. As a thousand TV shows have told us, "Anything you say can be used against you." Do not assume that if you do not talk to the police they will perceive that you have something to hide. The job of the police is to collect the facts. If they believe you have committed child abuse, they will arrest you.

If a police officer shows up at your center to talk with you, he or she is not required to read you your Miranda Rights ("You have a right to remain silent..."). You can ask the officer to leave, or you can have someone else in the room with you when questioned, or you can ask the officer to talk with your attorney. If the officer asks you to come to the police station to answer questions, you can refuse. You do not have to explain your reasons for why you are refusing. Even if you do go to the police station and answer some questions, you can change your mind at any time and refuse to answer further questions.

If you are arrested, you can also refuse to answer any questions. The best way to stop police questioning is to say, "I want to speak with an attorney." At that point, all questions must stop and anything you say after this point cannot be used against you. One reason it's a good idea to have another person with you whenever the police question you is that they can be a witness to your request for an attorney. If you agree to go to the police station to answer questions, the police can prevent you from having another person with you during the interview. This is why you usually don't want to go to the police station voluntarily.

Note: It is a good idea to develop a positive relationship with your local police before there is any accusation of child abuse. Meet with local officers and ask them what they will do if they receive an accusation of child abuse and what they would expect from your center. Share with the police your understanding of your responsibilities under the law and ask for advice on any questions you have about reporting child abuse.

Consulting an Attorney

An attorney can be helpful in many ways. He or she can coach you on how to respond to questions from investigators. An attorney can help you get your facts straight and speak clearly. He or she may help you think of facts you have not considered. Working with an attorney can definitely help you reduce the stress of an investigation.

If a parent is suing your center, it's likely that your business liability insurance policy will pay for any legal fees. However, your policy is unlikely to pay for an attorney to represent you in a criminal matter (where the consequence is you going to jail). In any case, it's always a good idea to contact your insurance agent whenever your program is under investigation.

Ideally, you want to consult with an attorney at the early stages of any criminal investigation of an injury. We recommend hiring an attorney before talking to the police. This may not be possible because many child care centers have difficulty paying for legal assistance. Contact your board of directors to see if any member can help you find an attorney. See Chapter 2 for more information about how to find and work with an attorney.

Suing Parents

Let's assume that a parent has made a false accusation of child abuse against your program. After the investigation clears your program, you may feel like you want to sue the parent (assuming you know who made the accusation). Without an independent witness who can testify that this parent knowingly made a false accusation, it will be extremely difficult for you to succeed in court. Consult with an attorney about your chances of success.

SEX OFFENDERS

Unfortunately, all children are at risk of exposure to sexual abuse. Besides complying with child abuse and neglect laws and monitoring your own employees, your center will also want to protect the children in your care from sex offenders. Talk to your local police officers about how to gain access to public records of sex offenders who live near your building. Some state laws prohibit sex offenders from living within a certain distance of a school or child care center. Assign a staff person to regularly check such public records to be sure no one is violating the law by living too close.

What if you discover that a parent of one of the children in your program is a sex offender? If the offender would be violating the law if he or she shows up at your program, you should alert your staff to call the police if he or she does appear. Even if the offending parent is not picking up his or her child, you can still legally refuse to provide care.

You could also terminate care when the offender does not have custody and lives separately from the child. Remember, it's legal to discriminate as long as the reason for the different treatment is not based on a person's protected class (race, sex, religion, etc.). Most child care centers would go out of their way to try to provide care for a child in a family with a sex offender, as long as they can do so in a way that does not put the children in their program at risk.

The health and safety of the children in your care is your most important mission. Establishing preventative policies will reduce the risk of injuries. When injuries do occur, handle them in a professional manner and seek legal help when necessary.

6 Minority Rights

Whose Differences Are Protected?

The law has long sought to find a balance between the rights of a few versus the rights of the many. To put a civil right to a majority vote would likely result in the right being abolished. Legislators and judges struggle with their responsibility to protect the rights of the minority with the expectations of the majority. Right now, proposed changes to our laws on minority rights are being passionately debated across the country.

BALANCING MINORITY AND MAJORITY NEEDS

How does this balancing dynamic play out in the everyday world of early childhood programs? As we consider the rights of immigrant children, English-language learners, LGBT children and families, and children with special needs, we will address the following:

- What are the rights of this group?
- How do these rights translate into everyday reality?
- What are our responsibilities as early childhood professionals?
- How do we apply this information to a case study?

In each instance, you will be invited to consider where you stand and what action you will take.

> *To protect those who are not able to protect themselves is a duty which everyone owes to society.*
>
> —Edward Macnaghten, English jurist, *Jenoure v. Delmege*, 1890

IMMIGRANTS IN AMERICA

The Statue of Liberty's promise is heartwarming: "Give me your tired, your poor, your huddled masses yearning to breathe free" (Lazarus, 1883). Unfortunately, U.S. immigration law reveals that as each new wave of immigrants acclimated, that group attempted to limit or outright deny access to the next wave of immigrants. Quotas were established for "undesirables" early on. Northern Europeans, for example, quickly sought to limit the influx of southern and eastern European immigrants.

> All too will bear in mind this sacred principle, that though the will of the majority is in all cases to prevail, that will, to be rightful, must be reasonable; the minority possess their equal rights, which equal laws must protect, and to violate which would be oppression.
>
> —Thomas Jefferson, 1st Inaugural Address, 1801

On the West Coast, where the San Francisco Bay Bridge serves as the welcoming icon, Asian immigrants, Chinese and Japanese in particular, have been felled by repressive immigration laws. In 1878, the U.S. Supreme Court prohibited Chinese immigrants from becoming naturalized citizens. Citizenship rights of Japanese American citizens during World War II were retracted overnight by our government. Japanese families in cities such as Seattle and San Francisco were unceremoniously rounded up, forced onto trains or buses, and deposited in internment "camps" bordered by barbed wire and armed guards. Today, legislators in states such as Arizona and Georgia want "illegal aliens" deported.

THINK ABOUT IT

What has been your family's history in this country? Was your heritage honored? How much of the "old ways" practiced by your ancestors have been lost, or continued? Would you describe your family's experience here more as a "melting pot" (fit in) or "tossed salad" (maintain your identity)?

We are not as a country near a resolution of these conflicting legal standards and practices. Were we to review the history of how citizens with special needs, English-language learners, and persons of diverse sexual orientations have been treated, we would see a similar twisting path.

As an early childhood leader, where do you stand on the rights of people and groups who are in the minority? Should we respect differences and ensure the rights of those who are not like the majority population, or should we require minorities to learn and practice the ways of the majority, leaving differences behind?

What Are Their Rights?

Jorge and Marisela Ramirez are two of the most eager-to-learn children you have ever met. The parents, who emigrated from Honduras when Jorge was a toddler, have worked two and sometimes three jobs apiece to maintain a comfortable rented home for Jorge and his baby sister, Marisela. When you asked Mr. Ramirez for required copies of the children's birth certificates, he gave you Marisela's. You hear that the family is terrified of being deported to their troubled country. Do you push for the birth certificates?

Both court rulings and the Equal Protection clause of our Constitution establish rights for children of illegal aliens, whether those children were born in America or elsewhere. Most notably:

- The U.S. Supreme Court struck down a Texas law prohibiting enrollment of illegal aliens in public schools (*Pyler v. Doe*, 457 US 202 [1982]).
- The federal McKinney-Vento Act prohibits public schools from turning away homeless or migrant children who lack birth certificates or proof of residency (Serrie, 2011).

On the other hand, the USA Patriot Act (2001) empowers the attorney general to take into custody and deport an alien who "is engaged in any other activity that endangers the security of the United States" (Title IV, 412).

Legal Mandates Translated into Everyday Reality

All children, regardless of citizenship documentation, have the same rights as U.S. citizens to receive a free public education. Any educational organization that benefits from federal funds such as food programs is considered to be a "public" institution. Most early childhood programs accept some form of federal funds.

Therefore, a child care center cannot turn a family away because the family is suspected to be in this country illegally. Similarly, social security numbers are not required for school enrollment at public schools or private schools that receive federal funding. In 1995, a California court held:

> Although federal law prohibits any person from concealing, harboring or shielding a known, undocumented immigrant from detection, this prohibition does not apply to school enrollment or education services and does not prevent educators or others from supporting undocumented students or connecting them with community advocates. However, educators should not interfere in Immigration and Customs Enforcement actions. (*League of Latin American Citizens v. Wilson*, 908 F. Supp. 755, 774, C.D. Cal. 1995)

California cases often set the precedent for other cases around the country. Children born in this country are U.S. citizens, regardless of their parents' citizenship. As a result of the Patriot Act, authorities can deport one or both parents. The children left behind can face many hardships, not the least of which is loss of a parent. Even if the parent does not fall under purview the Patriot Act, that parent may still be deported due to his or her illegal alien status.

Our Responsibilities as Early Childhood Professionals

Child care professionals can enroll and serve children and families who are not citizens. We are not required to report parents as illegal aliens. In fact, the NAEYC Code of Ethical Conduct (2005) instructs:

> We shall maintain confidentiality and shall respect the family's right to privacy, refraining from disclosure of confidential information and intrusion into family life. (*et seq.* P-2.9)

However, the Patriot Act (2001) mandates that child care programs cooperate with authorities if there is an ongoing investigation:

> The Attorney General (or any federal employee of a rank not lower than Assistant Attorney General) may seek an *ex parte* order requiring an educational institution to permit the Attorney General to collect any records in the possession of the institution "relevant to an authorized investigation" as long as there is "reason to believe" these records will contain relevant information. (Patriot Act 507)

Because state and federal laws are in flux on immigrant rights, stay up to date on your state's requirements.

Alabama, for example, enacted a law in the fall of 2011 requiring schools to "Collect and report to the state proof of a student's age, as well as a new provision requiring proof of where a child was born" (Serrie, 2011). Although courts in Arizona, Georgia, Indiana, and Utah have declared such laws unconstitutional, laws in other states (e.g., Alabama) prevail until courts overturn them.

Given this information, what would you do in the case of the Ramirez family? If you choose to follow the Alabama law, your choice may result in Jorge and his parents' deportation. You could, instead, seek the help of a local attorney to find how you can support or join in a lawsuit to overturn an unconstitutional law.

Case Study: Immigrant Family Rights

Felipe and Marie Montes and their three American-born children resided in North Carolina. Mr. Montes was deported to Mexico as an illegal alien after living in America for 9 years. His wife, Marie, the children's disabled mother, was unable to care for the children without Felipe's help. Their children were placed in foster care. Efforts are under way to reunite Mr. Montes with his children in Mexico (Wessler, 2012). What would you do if the Montes children were enrolled in your program?

First, know what your state law requires. If your state does not require you to document the citizenship of children and families, you need to question why your program's policy demands birth certificates. If you believe your policy is not in compliance with the law, work to change the policy. If state law requires you to obtain citizenship records, you might practice "civil disobedience." Join others who are contesting the unconstitutionality of the law.

ENGLISH-LANGUAGE LEARNERS

Another challenge for immigrant children is the language barrier. Does a child have the right to speak and learn in his or her native language, while at the same time learning English? NAEYC Core Values in the Code of Ethical Conduct ask us to commit to appreciating and supporting close ties between the child and the family. With English-language learners (ELs) we need to create an environment respectful of each child's heritage, including native tongue, while assisting the child in acquiring English-language proficiency.

What Are Their Rights?

Title I and Title III of the No Child Left Behind Act (NCLB) of 2006 include provisions for ELs. NCLB calls for all students to read and do math at grade level or better by 2014. NCLB uses its own acronym LEP (Limited English Proficiency) to identify EL children.

Title I outlines state standards, assessment, annual yearly progress reports, and other accountability requirements for EL students. Title III provides funding to state and local education agencies that are obligated by NCLB to increase the English proficiency and core academic content knowledge of LEP students. Under Title III, local school districts decide on the method of instruction to be used to teach EL students English, but it requires that instructional programs be scientifically proven to be effective. (See Appendix: Helpful Websites.)

In 2010, Illinois became the first state to mandate "that public schools with preschool programs offer a bilingual education to three- and four-year-olds who do not speak English" (Malone, 2010). Other states are following suit in establishing a process for the: (a) identification, (b) assessment, (c) provision of individualized learning plans, (d) assistance of EL specialists, (e) inclusion in the classroom, (f) involvement of parents, and (g) testing to determine progress, needs, and for "graduating" from the EL program.

Legal Mandates Translated into Everyday Reality

While most states scramble to draft and pass compliance standards for federal EL requirements, early childhood professionals are at work finalizing standards for our programs (see the Appendix for additional resources).

Karen Nemeth, an early childhood author whose specialty is ELs, summarizes what we need to do in *Many Languages, Building Connections: Supporting Infants and Toddlers Who Are Dual-Language Learners* (2012). (See the Appendix: Helpful Websites.)

While policy making is under way, let's examine how one New Hampshire school district with preschool programs, School Administrative Unit #39 (SAU #39), might provide a model for us in how to welcome EL students and families.

SAU #39's handbook includes a description of "content-based instruction," which aligns closely with early childhood principles. Content-based instruction for ELs:

- simulates the conditions and demands of the subject matter in the classroom;
- allows language learners to deeply engage with content;
- allows language learners to acquire the academic vocabulary and language skills needed for mainstream classroom work;

- enhances second-language acquisition by use of native language in the home; and
- strengthens familial and cultural bonds by use of native language in the home, which improves self-esteem and identity.

In addition:

- Students need to be proficient in all four English-language domains (listening, speaking, reading, and writing).
- ELs are proficient in English when they are able to participate at the level of their peers in the general education classroom.
- Planned, focused practice of a language is necessary to achieve the level of proficiency needed to be successful in the general education classroom (Anctil, 2011).

This New Hampshire school system's policy and practices compliance handbook was written by teacher and EL specialist Janine Anctil; it documents a systematic approach to establishing policies, procedures, and practices for EL efforts in your program. (See the Appendix: Helpful Websites.)

Engaging Families of EL Children

Enlisting family support for their children's acquisition of English-language skills is necessary for the child and school to be successful. Take a look at New Hampshire SAU #39's form for parental consent for the child to participate in an EL program.

PARENTAL PERMISSION FOR ENGLISH-SPEAKERS OF OTHER LANGUAGES (ESOL) SERVICES

SAU #39

Student Name _____

Date _____

I understand that after careful evaluation, it is recommended that my child receive extra services in the ESOL program in the SAU #39. School personnel have discussed this assignment with me and I understand the following:

- This service is part of the SAU #39's educational program assisting children who have been identified as "Limited English Proficient" by the W-APT screener as well as home and academic data collected.

(continued)

PARENTAL PERMISSION FOR ENGLISH-SPEAKERS OF OTHER LANGUAGES (ESOL) SERVICES (*continued*)

- My child will participate in the ESOL program, which helps him/her learn English, cultural background, and other academic skills that will improve reading, writing, and oral language skills.
- The ESOL teacher may work with my child one-on-one, in small groups, or within the context of the classroom.
- The ESOL teacher will work with the classroom teacher to determine targeted skills.
- I will be kept informed of my child's progress during the year.
- If I have any questions about the ESOL program at any time, I may contact the ESOL teacher at school.
- My child will be assessed annually using the ACCESS for ELs assessment, as required by New Hampshire Department of Education. This assessment will be used to determine my child's progress in English acquisition.
- I have the right to refuse services for my child at any time.
- If I decline services, I have the right to request to have my child re-enrolled in the ESOL program at any time.
- Even if I have declined services, my child will still be included in the annual ACCESS for ELs assessment and I will be informed of the results in the spring.

I have read and understand the above information.

_____ I give permission for my child to participate in the ESOL program.
_____ I decline ESOL services for my child at this time.

(My child will participate in the ACCESS for ELs, as required by law.)

Our Responsibilities as Early Childhood Professionals

Because we work with children at a critical age for their language development, early childhood leaders and programs need to establish EL policies and practices that lead to seamless assistance for children and their families.

In addition to the resources previously noted, World Class Instructional Design and Assessment (WIDA) provides thorough guidance for successfully establishing, implementing, and continuously assessing your program's EL efforts. WIDA explains its "can-do" philosophy: "We focus our attention on expanding students' academic language by building on the inherent resources of English-language learners (ELs) and accentuating the positive efforts of educators" (see Appendix: Helpful Websites).

Genevieve, believed to be around 4 years old, was both orphaned and traumatized by the earthquake in Haiti. Genevieve was found after 3 days under the rubble of her apartment building, the only survivor. Diagnosed with post-traumatic stress disorder (PTSD), Genevieve has not yet been able to form relationships with her non-French-speaking adoptive parents or teachers. You frequently see Genevieve whispering to dolls in the classroom. What are your responsibilities to Genevieve and what steps would you take to help her find her way?

Genevieve deserves our help on many levels. Traumatized children, with PTSD in particular, need professional assistance and loving support in healing from the disasters (external, internal, or both) they endured (Bruno, 2010). As part of your EL policy, provide links to reliable community agencies for counseling and other assistance. With the help of caring professionals, both Genevieve and her parents can begin to build trusting relationships. Once Genevieve feels safe and supported, she will learn more readily. Her language-development skills will follow her social and emotional development closely.

LGBT CHILDREN AND FAMILIES

Federal legislation does not specifically outlaw discrimination based on sexual orientation. This lack of definitively legislated rights places LGBT children and families in a more vulnerable position than the previous minority groups we examined. Because of this, you as a program leader are likely to be in a position to lead the way on how these children and their families are welcomed into your program.

What Are Their Rights?

We can find some basis in both related legislation and case law to support LGBT rights in Title IX of the Education Amendments of 1972 (Title 20 USC Sections 1681–1688). Title IX prohibits discrimination on the basis of sex in federally funded programs.

Case law interpreting Title IX's applicability to LGBT children has been supportive of their right to be free from discrimination. In 2000, the court in a Northern District of California case, *Ray v. Antioch Unified School District* (107 F. Supp.2nd 1165), held that a student, perceived to be homosexual by his fellow students who assaulted and harassed him, was allowed to bring suit under the protection of Title IX. This guarantee of the student's "standing" to sue is an important element in gaining civil rights.

To further shore up the rights of LGBT children from discrimination, the U.S. Department of Education's Office of Civil Rights (OCR) maintains that "sexual harassment directed at gay or lesbian students that is sufficiently serious to limit or deny a student's ability to participate in or benefit from the school's program constitutes sexual harassment prohibited by Title IX" (Revised Sexual Harassment Guidance, Harassment of Students by School Employees, Other Students or Third Parties, OCR, Jan.19, 2001).

Numerous states (including Iowa, Maine, Massachusetts, New York, Vermont, and Wisconsin) have enacted laws prohibiting discrimination in educational programs based on sexual orientation. Is your state among them? (See Appendix: Helpful Websites.)

Despite the fact that there is no federal law that prohibits discrimination based on sexual orientation in the private sector, the following states and the District of Columbia enacted laws prohibiting sexual-orientation discrimination in both public- and private-sector jobs: California, Connecticut, Hawaii, Illinois, Iowa, Maine, Maryland, Massachusetts, Minnesota, Nevada, New Hampshire, New Jersey, New Mexico, New York, Rhode Island, Vermont, Washington, and Wisconsin. Some additional states prohibit sexual-orientation discrimination in public workplaces only. These listings, although not applicable directly to children, indicate which states are trending against discrimination for sexual orientation of children.

For another predictor of the trend toward protecting LGBT rights, let's look at the status of the Defense of Marriage Act (DOMA). Section 3 of DOMA defines marriage for federal purposes as a union between a man and a woman. This section was deemed unconstitutional by a federal district court judge in 2010. Even though that case was appealed, Attorney General Eric Holder announced on February 23, 2011, that the U.S. Department of Justice (DOJ) would no longer defend Section 3 of DOMA, by direct order of the president.

Section 3 of DOMA does not prohibit states from recognizing same-sex marriages. Nor does DOMA require states to recognize same-sex marriages. As a result, a couple married in one of the states allowing same-sex marriage (currently Connecticut, Iowa, Massachusetts, New Hampshire, New York, Oregon, Vermont, Washington, and the District of Columbia) may not be recognized as a married couple in a different state. This means that Arkansas is not required to recognize the marriage of a couple legally married in Massachusetts, if that couple relocates to Arkansas.

Legal Mandates Translated into Everyday Reality

An estimated 2 million children are being raised by LGBT families. LGBT families live in 96% of counties in the United States, with the highest concentrations in Mississippi, Arkansas, Texas, Louisiana, Alabama, South Carolina, Wyoming, Oklahoma, Kansas, and Montana. Ironically, none of these states offers much legal protection for its LGBT families (Center for American Progress, 2011; Youngblood, 2011).

Can two people of the same sex legally be parents of their children? Because no federal law addresses legal parentage, federal laws defer to the state laws where the family resides:

- California allows a same-sex couple to be legal parents of a child. The parents will be referred to as "natural" or "adoptive" (National Center for Lesbian Rights).
- Same-sex couples are restricted from petitioning for second-parent adoption in North Carolina, Utah, Nebraska, Wisconsin, Ohio, and Kentucky ("Second-Parent Adoption Laws," 2012).
- Second-parent adoption is allowed in only 18 states and the District of Columbia: Washington, Oregon, California, Nevada, Colorado, Iowa, Illinois, Indiana, Pennsylvania, New York, Vermont, New Hampshire, Maine, Massachusetts, Rhode Island, Connecticut, New Jersey, and Delaware ("Second-Parent Adoption laws," 2012).
- Eight states have laws in place that support fostering by LGBT parents by restricting discrimination against them: California, Connecticut, Massachusetts, New Jersey, New York, Oregon, Rhode Island, and Wisconsin ("Foster Care Laws & Regulations," 2012).

Same-sex families do not qualify for Social Security, food stamps, public housing, health care, early childhood programs, or inheritance and tax benefits afforded to heterosexual families. Without this assistance from governmental safety nets, LGBT families must raise children as single-parent families without help. According to Youngblood (2011), "children raised in LGBT families are more than twice as likely to live in poverty."

Our Responsibilities as Early Childhood Professionals

Of the three minority groups we have looked at so far, LGBT children and their families are afforded the least legal protection. As a result, we as early childhood professionals need to look more to our Code of Ethics than to case law or legislation. NAEYC standards contemplate respect for all children and families.

NAEYC encourages us "to participate in building support networks for families by providing them with opportunities to interact with program staff, other families, community resources, and professional services" (Section II, I-2.7).

You may know someone who, for religious reasons, does not approve of anyone who is not heterosexual. As professionals, our religious beliefs can be practiced in our personal lives; however, in the workplace, all early childhood professionals need to "above all, do no harm" by respecting children and their families who are part of this minority.

Case Study: Addressing Concerns

Preschooler Winston adores one book above all others in his classroom. That book, *And Tango Makes Three,* describes a baby penguin, abandoned while not yet hatched out of his egg, and raised by two male penguins. Winston begs his grandparents to visit the zoo in New York City's Central Park so he can see Tango and his dads.

Mr. and Mrs. Twitchell, Winston's grandparents who are raising him, are deeply disturbed about this book. They believe this book, others like it, and your allowing LGBT families into Winston's class are all sinful. They threaten to sue your program for infringing on their rights if you don't remove all literature that acknowledges or supports LGBT practices. They inform you that their pastor and church is behind them 100%. What do you do?

In this, as in all other cases where family members take issue with program policy and practice, you, as leader, can begin by listening fully to the family's concerns. As you listen, ask yourself if you and the family can reach an agreement at a deeper level. For example, you and Winston's grandparents both want the best for Winston. You both appreciate his excitement about baby animals. Perhaps you can share other baby animal books with the Twitchells that they can read to Winston. Perhaps you could invite the Twitchells to join you on a field trip to the local zoo. Sometimes, practical answers shared with compassion can unthaw frozen dynamics.

However, if the Twitchells insist your program remove books and other resources that include LGBT families, you need to take action. The NAEYC Code (2005, 1) requires us to "respect the dignity, worth, and uniqueness of each individual (child, family member, and colleague)" and to "respect diversity in children, families, and colleagues." Your mission statement is likely also to support inclusion of all types of families. Even if your state laws are restrictive of LGBT rights, your program can take a supportive stance. If the family is still in strong disagreement with your stance, you could suggest programs, such as faith-based ones, where the Twitchells are likely to find others who agree with their beliefs.

CHILDREN WITH DISABILITIES

Historically, children with disabilities were subjected to pervasive exclusionary practices. Segregated into separate classrooms or isolated in special schools, children were labeled in ways that scarred their sense of self and their ability to learn.

What Are Their Rights?

The segregation of children with disabilities began to change in 1975 when Congress enacted the Education for All Handicapped Children Act, which gave disabled students rights to a more complete educational experience. This act has since iterated into IDEA, the Individuals with Disabilities Education Act of 2004. Any state that accepts federal funding comes under the auspices of IDEA.

Children protected by IDEA have a disability in one of these categories: mental retardation, hearing impairments, speech or language impairment, visual impairment, serious emotional disturbance, orthopedic impairments, autism, traumatic brain injury, other health impairments, or specific learning disability (Schimmel et al., 2010, p. 50).

Under IDEA, children must be provided with *free appropriate public education* (FAPE). IDEA requires educational organizations to provide "a basic floor of opportunity" for the student. This is not as high a standard as one that would require schools to maximize the child's learning potential (p. 51). Nonetheless, IDEA has advanced the rights of disabled children far beyond pre-1975 practices.

Under the protections of IDEA, children with disabilities must be provided with the following:

- The *least restrictive environment* or integration with other students as appropriate
- An *Individualized Education Program* (IEP) that spells out the plan for how the child and staff will work together to help the child meet learning goals
- *Related services,* such busing to transport the child to the program (courts have deemed medical services not included in "related services")

- *Accommodations,* such as sign language interpreters and properly equipped, accessible bathroom facilities
- *Due process for parents,* to ensure families are kept abreast of the school's efforts, their child's progress, and know their right to share and/or challenge how their child is being treated (p. 52)

Two other federal laws provide additional rights for children with special needs:

- Section 504 of the Rehabilitation Act of 1973 and Section 504 (added in 2000) are broader in scope than IDEA. Section 504 prohibits discrimination against the disabled by federally funded institutions. For example, a child in a wheelchair is likely to be covered by Section 504 even if he or she is not covered by IDEA.
- The ADA (1990) and the ADA as Amended (2009), as they apply to employees, are described in Chapters 8 and 9. Many of the same principles apply to the rights of children whose impairment "substantially limits one or more major life activities." The ADA incorporates Section 504 and expands its coverage to children at both public and private educational institutions. Specifically, the ADA requires schools to "provide access" for children to participate in school events, such as field trips.

Several cases have been heard at the federal district court level. Only one case, *Roberts v. KinderCare Learning Centers, Inc.* (1995), was decided at the appellate court level; all others were decided though settlements, many of which are confidential. In *Roberts v. KinderCare,* the court determined the child care organization was not required to provide a one-on-one assistant to meet the child's extensive needs (Wood & Youcha, 2009, p. 17).

Legal Mandates Translated into Everyday Reality

Almost every early childhood program serves children with disabilities. The laws ensure that these children receive the assistance they need to learn at their own pace. Integrating disabled children with other children enhances the experience of all children. Children who are used to being with children with special needs see such integration as a way of life.

The response of staff who work with disabled children can vary. Although teachers value the richness of the classroom experience, the same teachers may report exhaustion from the effort involved. Because the whole learning community at your program (children, parents, and staff) is affected by the inclusion of children with special needs, you as leader can take steps to make sure the inclusion process is a success.

Our Responsibilities as Early Childhood Professionals

Federal legislation is clear: early childhood programs must provide quality educational services and opportunities for children with special needs. Our programs do not have to put themselves out of business in the effort of accommodating. Nonetheless, we need to take all the steps we can to respect the rights of disabled children and to provide them with the best possible educational opportunities.

Continuous training is necessary to help staff stay current on new research and practices. Resources and links to services in the community must also be updated regularly. Common concerns and fears that you might need to address include:

- Teacher–children ratios
- Sufficient time for each child
- Safety for self and others
- Special equipment
- Fear of hurting the child with a disability
- Lack of knowledge about disabilities
- Uncertainty about how to teach a child with a disability
- Potentially negative reactions of the other children and parents (Wood & Youcha, 2009, p. 80)

Employees need reflective time to acknowledge and work through their feelings as well as what they are learning and what they need to learn. The process of working with children with disabilities, although at times exhausting, is also uplifting.

You will find helpful websites in the Appendix on how to structure your program to meet the needs of children with disabilities and their families.

Be honest with yourself and your staff about difficult questions as they emerge, including the following:

- What should be done if a child is violent and a threat to him- or herself or others?
- Will teachers have enough time for other children if the child with a disability needs significant attention?
- How can the curriculum be modified to challenge all the students, including students with special needs?
- How can you best support a teacher when the majority of his or her students have special needs?
- How can the dangers of staff burnout be prevented and/or remedied?

- What can you do to help a child and his or her family make a successful transition to elementary school?
- How will you deal with taunts or teasing by other children?
- At what point can a program decide it can no longer serve the child?

One resource that is particularly practical and useful is included in *Principals Teaching the Law: Ten Legal Lessons Your Teachers Must Know* (2010). Chapter 3 is devoted to helping teachers understand the rights and needs of special education students. You will find lesson plans, including exercises in how to conduct interactive workshops for your staff. Listen to a podcast of one of the authors, attorney Suzanne Eckes, at http://www.bamradionetwork.com/.

If possible, take your staff on an off-site retreat to rest, play, relax, and reflect upon the gifts and the challenges of working with children with disabilities. Simply creating a clearing in the woods lets the sunlight in and guarantees greater perspective.

Case Study: Working with Parents

Elgar's parents are overwhelmed by their son's difficult behavior. They worry they do not spend enough time with Elgar's baby sister, because they must be constantly vigilant about Elgar's temper. When Elgar is upset, he throws anything in sight. He bruised a classmate when he threw a book, and he wounded the family's trusting Labrador retriever with a hockey stick.

Elgar's IEP seems to be making a difference, but change is painstakingly slow. Elgar's teachers are in danger of burnout. Parents of Elgar's classmates complain that their children's education is hampered by his pressing needs. As the leader, what can you do?

Elgar and his family remind us how vital it is to forge honest, caring, and dynamic relationships. Listen with your heart to their concerns, while confirming you all want the best for Elgar. Ask what the family does to help Elgar cope effectively with challenges. Incorporate any of these practices that are professionally sound. Invite the family to observe Elgar's classroom behavior. Share with them Elgar's positive moments along with his troubling times. Invite the family to identify with you patterns in Elgar's behavior. Along the way, you stand to learn something, and the family, feeling your respect and acceptance, may be more open to additional assistance.

7 Privacy and Confidentiality in the Internet Age

We live at a time when our privacy is under assault. Some would say we have lost the battle. Our computers can be hacked into and personal information stolen. Identity theft is common. Even though our bank, health care provider, and credit card company issue privacy policies, we are not reassured.

Parents of children enrolled at your child care center are also worried about their privacy and the privacy of their children. When they approach you about enrolling their child, they have a high expectation that their family's privacy will be protected.

Your center should be no less concerned about maintaining privacy and confidentiality. You cannot operate effectively unless you keep information about the families strictly confidential. Parents need to feel confident that your center shares a common interest in privacy. If this confidence is broken, parents may be reluctant to share information about their children (health information, home life problems, etc.) that can inhibit your ability to keep children safe and provide the best possible care.

How can your child care center protect the privacy and maintain the confidentiality of the families you serve? In this chapter we will discuss your ethical and legal duties concerning privacy, give examples of how to address common privacy concerns, look at special challenges from the Internet, and cover unique issues in dealing with confidentiality and your staff.

ETHICAL AND LEGAL ISSUES

The NAEYC Code of Ethical Conduct calls upon child care centers to "develop written policies for the protection of confidentiality and the disclosure of children's records." It also requires familial consent before the release of such records, unless state laws mandate their disclosure. Cases of abuse or neglect are an exception (P-2.12). Your state child care licensing rules may address this issue by declaring that children's records are confidential.

Virginia law says: "Staff and children's records shall be treated confidentially" (22VAC15-30-70).

Pennsylvania law says: "Child records are confidential and shall be stored in a locked cabinet. A facility person may not disclose information concerning a child or family, except in the course of inspections and investigations by agents of the Department" (Section 3270.183).

Surprisingly, not all states address the issue of privacy. When they do, they often detail what records you must keep (enrollment, health, incident reports, etc.) and who has access to them. In most cases, the rules will specify that such records are confidential and may be shared only with specific agencies (e.g., licensing, child protection services, and the police). State laws may also direct you to save records for a specific period of time or destroy them under certain conditions.

What about collecting information from parents that you are not required to collect? Many centers ask information about families at the time of enrollment to help make the child more comfortable as part of a smooth transition. Such questions might be: What holidays do you celebrate? What nicknames do you use? Who lives at home?

When collecting this personal information you should restrict access to those who need to know (classroom teacher) and take measures to ensure that it's not accidentally released. When children leave your program, such personal information should be destroyed.

Do you enjoy collecting information from parents, filing these records, keeping them safe, and keeping track of who is authorized to see them? We didn't think so. Although this work may seem far removed from the job of caring for children, failure to follow your state law can quickly get you into trouble. Violation of your compact with parents to keep their information confidential will likely anger them and could lead to them leaving your center, bad-mouthing you to other parents on the Internet, or suing you.

Your first step in addressing the issue of privacy and confidentiality is to share with parents your obligations under your state's licensing rules. Next, you should develop a general privacy policy and discuss it. Lastly, you should closely monitor the collection and release of parent/child information to make sure that no one (the public, other parents, and your staff) is able to gain unauthorized access to it.

COMMON PRIVACY CONCERNS

All parents expect you to keep any information about their children or their family strictly confidential. They don't want information released to anyone without their permission. They understand that you have an obligation to share information with appropriate agencies for the protection of their children, but they will react strongly to any unauthorized release of their names, addresses, phone numbers, and so forth.

You may be surprised to discover that your program is inadvertently sharing information about the families you care for. Do you have photographs of children posted in your classrooms or on your marketing materials or newsletters? Are the names of the children posted on classroom bulletin boards, cubbies, or artwork?

These are common practices in many child care centers, but they are a violation of a family's privacy. How so? Other parents can see this information, as well as strangers visiting your program or reading your materials. You should not assume that parents will agree that it is okay for anyone to know that their child is enrolled in your center.

How about this situation: Peter Hands, who does not have legal or physical custody of his child, contacts you asking for his child's attendance records. As discussed in Chapter 4, you should not release a child to a noncustodial parent. As a confidentiality issue, you should not share any information with a noncustodial parent.

Privacy Policy

The way to handle these common issues is to prepare a general privacy policy and a general permission form. Here's a sample privacy policy:

THE ABC CHILD CARE CENTER PRIVACY POLICY

The ABC Child Care Center will keep all records and information about your family strictly confidential and private. We will abide by our state's privacy laws and will release records or information about your family only when required by law. This includes releasing information to the child care licensing department, child protection agency, police, and health care professionals. Other than these legal requirements, we will release records or information about your family only with your written permission.

The director of the ABC Child Care Center will decide which staff may have access to confidential information about your child. The following records

---

(continued)

THE ABC CHILD CARE CENTER
PRIVACY POLICY (*continued*)

of your child are available for your inspection at any time: enrollment forms, medical records, immunization records, attendance records, assessment records, and incident reports. Contact the director to set up a time to view these records.

Parental Responsibilities

We forbid the taking of any pictures or videos (in whatever format) by parents (or anyone else) of the children in our program.

Common Practices

Below is a list of common practices we follow that may raise an issue for you about privacy. Please review these practices and initial each item to which you consent. If you do not consent, we will not share the information about your child.

- We may post photographs of your child in the classroom. _____ (I approve)
- We have a photo album of our program that may include a photo of your child. Prospective parents would be able to view this album. _____ (I approve)
- We may post the name of your child on his/her cubbie. _____ (I approve)
- We may post the name of your child or your name on classroom bulletin boards. _____ (I approve)
- We may post photos of your child in our program-marketing literature or newsletter. _____ (I approve)
- We may post artwork or other craft activities in the classroom that identify your child by name. _____ (I approve)
- We maintain a video surveillance camera in your child's classroom that will be shared only with staff (for training purposes) and with authorized authorities (if requested). _____ (I approve)

This permission is granted through one year from the date below.

Signed on this date _____

Parent signature _____

Parent signature _____

Notice that we included asking for permission for some specific practices in a general privacy policy. This can help save you a lot of time by not having to track down parents later for their permission.

By having parents sign this simple permission form at the time of enrollment, you can address many potential problems at once. As new issues arise, you will need to seek specific written permission.

For example, the local news station contacts you and wants to send over a camera crew to take some pictures/video of children to accompany a story about the latest child care issue (state cutbacks, new study on child development, etc.). Before agreeing to this, you will need to have written permission from every parent whose child is photographed.

Your response would be the same if one of the parents in your program visited her child during lunch and wanted to take pictures. No parental permission, no pictures. It's best to have a general policy that prohibits the taking of any photos or videos by parents in your center. Trying to get permission from all the families is time consuming.

Having an ending date on such a policy is a good idea because it requires you to revisit the parents to make sure they still agree with the permission they have granted.

Release of Information About Parents

Parent Bobby Yang approaches you and says, "We're having a big birthday party for my son Victor at our home in two weeks! I'd like the names and addresses of the other parents in my child's classroom so I can mail them an invitation." You reply, "Your party sounds great, but I can't release any information about the other parents in our program to you. It's against our privacy policy, which you have a copy of." You may or may not want to propose these alternatives: Allow the parent to drop off copies of the invitation on a table in the entry area, take copies of the invitation and put them in the cubbies for the parents to pick up, or make an announcement of the party on the classroom bulletin board or newsletter or on your website.

Parent Sonia Lopez tells you, "I was talking with the mother of Ingrid last night and I forgot to write down her phone number. I'm going out of town and won't see her for a few days and I'd like to talk to her again. Could you give me her phone number?" You reply, "No, but if you give me a number you can be reached at, I will pass it on to Ingrid's mother and tell her to contact you."

Release of Information About Children

On Monday you get a call from a person who says, "I'm Harriet Olsen, a counselor from the Abraham Elementary School. The parents of Natalie Johnson told us she is enrolled in your child care program. Is that right? I'm asking because I'd like to come over and visit Natalie's classroom so I can observe her. We are dealing with some behavioral issues and we would like to coordinate our efforts with your staff." You reply, "Our policy is not to release any information about the children in our program, which includes answering questions about who is enrolled. Ask Natalie's parents to talk to us directly and we can then decide the proper course of action."

Your center should have a policy about outside people entering your classrooms. The policy should require notification of the other parents in the classroom, along with written permission. This would be relatively easy to do when an outside person, such as a magician, puppeteer, or music teacher, came to your center. But, what about potential clients touring your building? You may want to include this scenario in your privacy policy to ensure that parents enrolled in your program are okay with this. You may also want to ask prospective parents to respect the privacy of the families enrolled in your program. You could ask those touring your program to sign a simple statement: "I agree not to share any information with third parties about the children and their families enrolled in the ABC Child Care Center."

Terri, a toddler room teacher, says to you, "I'm having problems with one of the children in my room, Billy Harmer. He has been acting out the past several days, occasionally hitting other children. None of the techniques I've used to address this have worked. I'd like to talk with the county health care worker and ask her for help. I'm also getting questions from the other parents of the children about who is hitting their children. Any advice?" You respond, "Go ahead and ask the health worker for advice. Just don't share Billy's name. Tell the other parents that you will not share names and that you are following our policy about confidentiality and are following procedures to address the problem."

Under the Americans with Disabilities (ADA) law, information about children with disabilities is protected. Discussing a child's disabilities without parental written permission is a breach of confidence and can result in a lawsuit. Therapists and other specialists who come into the program to work with the child should have written permission from the parents to talk about the child with the teacher if they are not part of the Individualized Education Program (IEP). You should decide how many staff need to be privy to all the child's medical information as well as the IEP documents.

School Records

Under the Federal Educational Rights and Privacy Act (FERPA), any early childhood education program that receives federal funding of any kind (including directly or indirectly through a state or local grant program) must protect the privacy of student education records. The law also gives parents the right to inspect, review, and petition change of these records. Schools must have written permission from the parent in order to release any information from the student's records (with some exceptions). (See Data Quality Campaign in references.)

Slander

You receive a call from Cynthia, another center director in your city, who says, "We are interviewing Marian Ward, who is interested in enrolling her child in our program. She's told us that her child Gretchen was previously in your center. She has given your center as a reference and I'd like to ask you a few questions. Can you tell us if Marian always paid on time and if you had any serious issues in caring for Gretchen?"

In this situation you need to protect both the privacy of the parent and the child. Without written permission from the parent, you should not answer any questions or even acknowledge that you cared for this family. You respond, "Because of our privacy policy, we don't release the names of any families who are currently enrolled or have been previously enrolled in our center. I cannot say anything more unless we were to receive written permission from Marian to talk with you."

What do you do if Marian does send you written permission to talk with Cynthia? Here you need to understand the potential legal pitfalls of slander. Defamation occurs when you make a negative statement about another person that is false and damages that person's reputation in the community. If the statement is made verbally it is slander; if it's made in writing it's libel. The law does not require you to answer any questions about past clients. Many child care centers have a policy that forbids them from giving any information about past clients to another child care program.

If you do give out information about past clients (with their permission), you want to avoid the risk of committing slander. Stick to the facts. If it's true, it's not slander. So, you could say, "According to our records, Marian was late in making her payments six times during the one year she was at our program." Don't say, "Marian was a deadbeat, irresponsible parent." You could say, "We had three parent conferences with Marian about some problems Gretchen had in socializing with the other children." Don't say, "Gretchen was always out of control and our staff could barely manage her."

Because it may be difficult to walk the line between stating facts and slander, you may want to offer only the statement, "We would/ would not provide care again for this family."

Giving References to Other Child Care Centers

You may be in the position of being asked to give out the names of other child care centers to parents who cannot use your services (you have a waiting list, or don't care for infants). The best practice is to give parents the name of your local child care resource and referral agency, rather than give out names of individual centers. This is the path that carries no legal risks.

If you do decide to give out names of other centers, you want to avoid the appearance of giving the parent a recommendation. If the parent has a bad experience with the center you referred, she may try to sue you, claiming that you recommended the center and she relied on your recommendation.

Instead, make referrals, not recommendations. This means giving out the names of more than one center each time (if possible). Limit what you say: "Here are the names of several centers that may be able to help you." Do not praise the other program ("This center will be perfect for your child.") or offer information that may no longer be true ("This center has a nurse on staff.").

INTERNET CHALLENGES

The Internet offers expanding opportunities to promote your child care program and help children learn. At the same time, it poses a growing threat to the privacy of everyone. Your program needs to have a privacy policy about the sharing of photographs and videos of the children in your program on your website, YouTube, Facebook, Flickr, and so on. Your policy should also cover the sharing of information on the Internet by your staff.

Because of the widespread use of the Internet, it's a good idea to have a separate Internet privacy policy. Here is a sample:

INTERNET PRIVACY POLICY

In addition to our general policy on privacy, the ABC Child Care Center has adopted this Internet Privacy Policy to protect the privacy of its clients. We will not share any information on the Internet about the current or past children and families enrolled in our program without the written permission of the parents.

This includes the posting of names, contact information, photographs, videos, audio, or other likeness of children or family members on our website,

Facebook page, Twitter, YouTube, or any other location that could be distributed through the Internet. This includes the sharing of information through texting on cell phones. We have also adopted a confidentiality policy with the employees of our center that prohibits them from sharing any information about children or family members on the Internet.

Parents are asked to sign a copy of this policy indicating that they have read and received a copy.

Signed on this date _____

Parent signature _____

Parent signature _____

When you do want to use information about a child on the Internet, you should create a parent permission form, such as this example:

INTERNET PARENT WAIVER AND RELEASE FORM

By signing this waiver and release form, I/we authorize the _____ _____ (*name of child care program*) to use photographs, audio, or video identified below of _____ (*name of child*) in the production of any marketing materials, newsletters, websites, Facebook page, videotapes, and any other advertisements or promotions that _____ (*name of child care program*) may decide to develop, now or in the future.

Further, by signing this waiver and release, I/we certify that I/we am/are the legal parent or guardian of the child identified above.

Parent/Guardian _____

Parent/Guardian _____

Date _____

Description of Photograph(s) and/or Video(s) _____

_____

The problem with the Internet is that once information is posted there, it can remain public indefinitely. A photograph of a child taken on a cell phone can be instantly transmitted to another person, or uploaded to Facebook or many other websites. Likewise, if you send a group email to parents allowing them to see the email addresses of everyone else, you have violated confidentiality.

This is not to say that everything about the Internet is bad. Far from it! You and your staff can use the Internet to learn about child development, appropriate learning activities, and to communicate directly with other child care programs from around the world. You can use the Internet to increase your communication with parents and involve them more closely with the education of their children. You can post your policies and forms and link to parenting resources on your center's website. You can use sites such as YouTube, Flickr, or Shutterfly to share video or photographs of children in a secure environment where only parents have access. You can create password-protected groups on Facebook where staff and parents can talk about what their children are learning. When creating these secure sites on the Internet, you should still seek parental permission and have a policy that prohibits parents from sharing this information (including photographs and video) with others. Finally, you can use the Internet to promote your center by using social media sites and online classified ads, and all for little, if any, money.

WHEN YOUR CENTER'S REPUTATION IS ATTACKED ON THE INTERNET

Unfortunately, there is another downside of the Internet; parents can post negative comments and reviews of your child care program. Although the free sharing of information and opinion is a value we uphold, negative opinions and false statements can seriously damage your center's reputation.

There are a number of Internet sites where parents can post reviews of your center. Although the number of reviews on these sites is currently very small, it is likely to grow over time. There are also a number of social media sites and parent forums where parents may post negative comments about your center. Ask the parents in your program what social media sites and forums they use and monitor these sites. (See Appendix: Helpful Websites.)

Here are the steps to take to protect your center:

Contact Your Child Care Licensor. Parents (or others) who make damaging statements on the Internet may later file a complaint with licensing. Explain to your licensor what was said and correct any false statements. Ask the licensor to make a note of your conversation. Licensors are less likely to take seriously a parent complaint if they have heard from you first.

Read the Terms and Conditions of These Websites. See if the parent is violating them. If so, report it to the site. Respond to the online criticism by asking other parents in your program to write a positive review on the same site where the negative comments appeared. Note that some parents may be reluctant to be drawn into such a dispute and may not want to know about what was said about your program! It's best to ask only parents whom you know well for help.

Consult with an Attorney. If the parental comment is particularly disturbing, you may be tempted to think about suing the parent. It is difficult, however, to sue someone for libel (spreading of false, written statements that damage your center's reputation). Proving that the parent knew his or her statement was false can be a daunting task and it will cost you time and money to hire an attorney. You may want to consult with an attorney for advice about whether or not to follow up with a lawsuit or a warning to the parent to stop.

Consult These Rating Sites on a Regular Basis. See if parents are making comments about your program. You may want to ask some of the parents to make positive comments about your program on these sites before you see any negative comments! You can also monitor your center's online reputation by Googling your center's name on a regular basis to see what others are saying about your program. You can also hire companies that can monitor and protect your reputation for a fee (see Appendix: Helpful Websites).

LICENSING RECORDS

A growing trend is for state child care licensing agencies to post licensing inspection records and any history of licensing violations on the Internet. Depending on what is posted, this can create a problem for your center. Prospective parents might see these reports/violations and assume your program is not suitable for their child. The problem with such postings is that parents will have little, if any, context to help them interpret what they read. For example, a parent who sees that your program was cited four times in the past 2 years for various licensing violations will not be aware that perhaps other centers in your community fare much worse.

What can you do about this? Look on a regular basis to see what is posted on the Internet by child care licensing about your center. At the same time, check out what is posted about your chief competitors to see how your program compares. When a prospective client says to you, "I'm concerned about the four licensing violations about your center that are posted on the Internet," you can reply, "We immediately addressed those issues and are currently in full compliance with all licensing rules. We've compared our record with the record of other child care centers in our area. We averaged one violation a year over the past 5 years, which is better than the average of three violations a year by the other centers. In addition, none of our violations involved safety issues affecting children, whereas other centers did have such violations on their record."

STAFF ISSUES

Your staff plays an important role in helping protect the privacy and confidentiality of the families in your program. Their actions are a reflection of the professional image you want your center to project, whether or not they are at work. You will need to give direction to help your staff handle a variety of situations:

- A staff member hears personal information about a parent or child and is tempted to share it with other staff or friends through social media.
- A staff member takes pictures of children and sends them via cell phone to past staff members.
- A staff member develops a personal relationship with a parent outside of the center hours.

The first step in involving staff in your center's responsibilities to maintain confidentiality is to develop a policy. You want all staff members, including the cook, driver, teacher, substitute, and director, to sign your policy.

ABC CHILD CARE CENTER STAFF CONFIDENTIALITY POLICY

The ABC Child Care Center has a strong commitment to protect the privacy of the families we serve and to maintain the confidentiality of the information we collect on these families. This policy is part of our commitment as early childhood professionals. By following our confidentiality policy, we will promote and maintain positive relationships with our families that will build trust.

- We will keep all records and information about the children and parents we are in contact with strictly confidential and private. We will maintain confidentiality both while working as employees of the center as well as when we are not employees.
- We will abide by our state's privacy laws and will release records or information about children or families only when required by law. This includes releasing information to the child care licensing department, child protection agency, police, and health care professionals. Other than these legal requirements, we will release records or information about children and family only with parental written permission.
- We will not share with others personal information we may hear about children or parents with other staff or with anyone outside of the center. We will not pass on, or participate in, gossip about children or their families.
- We will not take pictures of children or parents without the approval of the director of the center. We will not share pictures of children or parents with staff or anyone outside our center. This includes posting pictures on the Internet or sending them via cell phone, or any other means of communication.
- Cell phone use by staff will be prohibited while in the company of children, unless authorized by the director.
- We will not post negative comments on Twitter, Facebook, text messages, or on any Internet sites about children, families, other staff, or the ABC Child Care Center.
- Written information about children and parents will be kept confidential and access to their files is limited to persons authorized by the director.
- Our pledge of confidentiality extends to the time when we are no longer employed by the center.
- Failure of staff to abide by this policy can lead to disciplinary action, up to and including termination.

Date _____

Signed _____

We encourage you to put in the parent enrollment packet either a copy of this policy or a mention that a copy is available for review. Letting parents know that you have a clear and strong internal confidentiality policy is a good way to promote a successful partnership. Encourage parents to talk with you if they have any concerns about privacy or confidentiality. You should also ask parents to respect the privacy of other families as well as your staff.

Does having such a policy infringe on the First Amendment rights of staff? No. You can institute policies that protect your program from staff members who make statements or take action that threaten your center's mission. A teacher who puts on her Facebook page comments that are critical of children, families, other staff, or your program can be disciplined or fired.

We recommend including a discussion about your center's confidentiality policy with all employees before they are hired. Conduct regular trainings on this topic throughout the year and facilitate discussions with staff about your policy. A good way to introduce discussions is to pose questions: What should I do if I overhear another staff person gossiping about a parent? Should I accept a parent's invitation to attend her child's birthday party at the child's home on a weekend? I overheard a parent talking about getting a divorce. Should I share this with the child's teacher?

Although there are no federal laws that require you to keep job performance records confidential, it would be best practice to do so. Release of such information can lead to a defamation lawsuit. The NAEYC Code of Ethics says, "We shall maintain confidentiality in dealing with issues related to an employee's job performance and shall respect an employee's right to privacy regarding personal issues" (P-3C.9).

We all recognize the importance of protecting the privacy and maintaining the confidentiality of children, their families, and your staff. By adopting some written policies, gaining parent permission when necessary, and being alert to potential problems, you can help ensure that you are offering a safe place for everyone.

8 Employee Hiring Process

Ethical and Legal Policies

You can demonstrate our field's professionalism to applicants through sound hiring practices. These practices attract the best employees and enlarge a program's recruiting capability. Our early childhood applicant pool is rarely as deep or as clear as we need it to be. To say that professionals in our field are underpaid is beyond an understatement. Job offers with better pay and benefits are hard to turn down.

Throughout the hiring process, even with these pressures, we need to take a stand to hire the best. By developing trustworthy personnel processes, we attract the best applicants and prevent lawsuits related to hiring. Let's consider the following:

1. Limitations of current procedures for getting substantive references
2. A Hold Harmless policy to remedy these limitations
3. Job descriptions that focus on the task, not on an applicant's physical attributes
4. Interview questions that honor applicants' rights while gleaning information on applicants' skills and knowledge
5. Equal opportunity for all applicants, including those with disabilities
6. How to make reasonable accommodations without "undue hardship"
7. The expanded list of major life processes in the Americans with Disabilities Act as Amended (ADAAA)
8. Cultural differences affecting applicants

Some of the issues in this chapter may surprise you. The law and our individual sense of morality do not always shake hands.

OBTAINING REFERENCES OF SUBSTANCE

Director Isaiah, interviewing applicants for infant room lead teacher, is flabbergasted. Every time he calls for a reference, he hears, "We share only whether the person worked for us and her/his employment dates."

Isaiah needs to know about classroom management skills, creativity with curriculum, and ability to work with children with special needs. "How am I supposed to find the best candidate when I can't get real information?" Isaiah fumes.

State licensing regulations as well as NAEYC standards require employers to check references on applicants prior to hiring. Directors, seeking the most qualified person for the position, need details about the applicant's past job performance.

NAEYC Accreditation Criterion 10.E.02 requires that "hiring procedures ensure that all employees in the program (including bus drivers, bus monitors, custodians, cooks, clerical and other support staff) who come into contact with children in the program or who have responsibility for children. . . have provided personal references. . . ." Some state licensing agencies require verification by references. For example, in California, "references must be used to verify experience" of directors and teachers (CA Regulations 101215.1[h][1]; 101216.1[c][1][C]).

Michigan lists "check references" as a step in hiring child care staff (Michigan Family Independence Agency, 2004).

Most directors report they cannot obtain meaningful, substantive information when calling former bosses for applicant references. Let's look at what might help.

QUIZ

Preschool teacher Mari quit before Director Bernadette put her on probation. Mari failed to use developmentally appropriate practices and was frequently late for work. Unbeknownst to Bernadette, Mari, applying for another teaching position, gave Bernadette's name as a reference. When Mari's potential new director, Isaiah, calls Bernadette to ask, "What do you think of Mari's performance as a teacher?" Bernadette should do which of the following?

a. Share only the dates of Mari's employment.
b. Respond "yes" or "no" to the question: "Would you rehire Mari?"
c. Confide "off the record" that Mari was a disappointment.
d. Say, "In my professional opinion, I do not recommend Mari."
e. Say, "I'll check our files to see if Mari gave us written permission to provide a reference."

Current Policies on Providing Employee References

Check your program's policy on providing references on former employees. You are likely to find something like: "We provide only the dates of the person's employment in confirming he or she worked here."

Where does this leave Bernadette? At best, she can provide the dates of Mari's employment, job title, and final salary. She cannot reveal that Mari was a substandard employee. If Bernadette were to say more, she would violate policies. She may also become vulnerable to a lawsuit from Mari for slander (willfully and orally harming another person's reputation in the community).

In some cases, the policy on providing references might include this additional clause: "In response to the question, 'Would you rehire this person?' you can answer either yes or no." If this were her program's policy, Bernadette could respond with a simple "no" to Isaiah's question: "Would you rehire Mari?"

What if the potential new employer, Isaiah, is impressed with Mari's interview? Having no further information to back up Bernadette's "no," Isaiah hires Mari. Once hired, Mari shows up late for work and expects toddlers to behave like kindergarteners. Parents complain to Isaiah. Meanwhile, Bernadette frets, "I wish I could have told him the truth!"

Holding Former Employers Harmless for References

Consider how the following sample policy can help administrators give and receive useful employee references:

"HOLD HARMLESS" CONSENT TO PROVIDE REFERENCE

I, _____ (employee name), agree to hold _____ (program title) harmless for any reference that program provides to a potential employer of mine.

Specifically, I authorize that these areas of my job performance may be openly discussed (Initial selected areas):

— Classroom management
— Developmentally appropriate practices
— Relationships with parents/families
— Curriculum expertise and creativity
— Inclusiveness
— Timeliness
— Attendance
— Taking initiative
— Respect for diversity
— Team player

(continued)

"HOLD HARMLESS" CONSENT TO PROVIDE REFERENCE (*continued*)

— Other, (Specify): _____

_____ Date _____

(Employee's name, position)

_____ Date _____

(Administrator's name), (title)

Imagine how this document transforms the process for giving references. Mari completes the form, authorizing Bernadette to provide a reference about the areas Mari initials. When Isaiah asks Bernadette about Mari's job performance, Bernadette can share her professional opinion about Mari's performance in any areas initialed.

"In my professional opinion, Mari's classroom expertise in developmentally appropriate practices is lacking," Bernadette can tell Isaiah. If Bernadette is asked to comment on an area Mari did not initial, such as timeliness or attendance, Bernadette can say, "I do not have the employee's permission to comment on those areas."

Because Mari has consented to Bernadette's providing an honest evaluation of her performance, Mari holds Bernadette and her program harmless for providing that reference. Everyone benefits: Isaiah makes an informed hiring decision; Bernadette provides her honest professional opinion; Mari controls the areas of her performance that can be discussed; and, above all, children are protected.

Here is another use of the Hold Harmless Consent to Provide Reference policy. Suppose you are called to provide a reference on a former employee who has given your name as a reference but has not completed the Hold Harmless form. Email a blank form. The potential employer can then ask the applicant to complete the form and submit it to you. If the applicant submits the form to you, he or she empowers you to provide a substantive reference. If the former employee/applicant refuses to complete the Hold Harmless form, he or she will need to explain that decision to the potential employer.

Sharing Hold Harmless Consent to Provide Reference Forms with Staff

Directors can ask teachers to complete these forms at any time during employment and as part of the exit interview. Requiring a new employee to sign this form on the day he or she is hired may not be the best practice, however. If new employees say they are not comfortable with the form, they may worry about looking bad on their first day. Employees can claim they felt coerced to complete the form. Similarly, if you wait until the employee resigns or is terminated, your chances of getting a useful, completed form are unlikely.

> **THINK ABOUT IT**
>
> If you incorporate a Hold Harmless Consent to Provide Reference policy, when would you want employees to complete the form? At hiring, every six months, or when the employee departs?

Consider introducing the form periodically over the year. Discuss the form's value to the program and to each teacher's future. Teachers who have been on the job for a while and know where they stand will be more willing to complete and sign the form. Reintroducing the form to employees periodically serves as a valuable self-assessment tool. You, as supervisor, gather information on how to support the employee's professional development.

Case Study: Contacting References

Head preschool teacher Nazareth does not trust Gina, her former director at Little Darlings Academy, to provide a positive reference. Nazareth does not include Gina on her list of references. During her interview, Nazareth mentions her past employment at Little Darlings. Can Isaiah, the interviewing director, call Gina at Little Darlings to ask about Nazareth's performance? If Gina is called, what can she say?

Decide if completing the form is mandatory for your program. What do you do if an employee "reserves the right" not to sign the form? If you require completion of the form, you will need to take disciplinary action if a teacher fails to comply with program policy. If completing the form is optional, you provide your teachers with more leeway. You also restrict your ability to provide a substantive reference on every employee.

> **THINK ABOUT IT**
>
> How do you feel about your current policy on providing references? If you decide to institute the Consent to Provide References policy, what challenges will you face? How might this new policy affect quality in your program and the profession?

DRAFTING JOB DESCRIPTIONS

Traditionally, job descriptions list measurable requirements such as: "Must be able to lift 20 pounds." True enough, requirements that are measurable lead to an objective set of standards for fairness. Passage of the ADA (Americans with Disabilities Act) in 1990, and its more recent iteration, ADAAA (Americans with Disabilities Act as Amended, January 1, 2009), changes that standard for fairness.

The ADA's intent is to provide people who "are otherwise qualified" for the job equal opportunity to apply for, be hired, and enjoy working on the job. For years, people who are "otherwise qualified" have been discriminated against by not getting hired or even interviewed for positions. My sister Karen, an attorney who walked with a cane due to multiple sclerosis, said: "If I interview at a law firm and they see my cane, they'll find a reason not to hire me." Do you think her assessment of potential bias was accurate?

THINK ABOUT IT

Review your current job descriptions. Evaluate the function or tasks that need to be performed. Identify statements that focus on physical attributes. Change those statements to identify the task to be performed.

To reflect the new standards set by the ADA, many of us need to update our job descriptions and hiring practices. Job descriptions that require a physical attribute, such as the ability to lift 20 pounds, might discriminate against applicants with disabilities. That job description alone may discourage an applicant with a disability. Instead of "must be able to lift 20 pounds," the requirement may be worded as "must be able to diaper a baby appropriately" or "must be able to evacuate children safely and promptly in an emergency." This modification may make a difference in who applies to work for you.

WRITING JOB-INTERVIEW QUESTIONS

Interview questions must meet at least two standards:

1. Is every applicant asked the same questions?
2. Are applicants allowed to demonstrate their ability to meet the "functional requirements of the job"?

In the past, hiring interviews were informal. The interviewer was free to create questions as he or she went along. Not everyone had the chance to answer the same questions. Many people were hired without being interviewed. They got the job because of whom they knew. Before laws changed, jobs did not have to be posted and hiring practices were not scrutinized for fairness. Using a consistent set of interview questions gives applicants a fairer chance to demonstrate their qualifications.

ASKING APPROPRIATE INTERVIEW QUESTIONS

Equal employment law requires directors to treat each applicant for a position fairly, regardless of race, religion, age, gender, disability, or (in most cases) national origin. When interviewing possible employees, directors are required to give each person equal opportunity to respond to the same questions.

Jason's application for preschool teacher indicates he can perform the job functions. His associate's degree in early childhood is from a nearby college. In his cover letter, Jason notes his military service in Iraq strengthened his desire to work with young children. When Jason arrives for the interview with a smile, he shrugs off his coat. Jason's right arm appears to have been amputated. The interviewing team becomes anxious about what they can ask. What could you do in advance to help all parties feel welcome and prepared?

If an interviewer were to use different questions for different applicants, he or she could be accused of favoring one applicant over another. Most directors use a written set of interview questions and scenarios that is consistent for each applicant.

Can the Applicant Perform the Essential Functions of the Job?

When directors interview applicants, they seek to hire the person best qualified to "perform the essential functions of the job." The Childcare Law Center's booklet (1996) "Employing People with Disabilities: The Americans with Disabilities Act and Child Care" defines *essential functions* as:*"The tasks and duties that describe the job, but only those that are essential to the performance of the job."* Essential functions of the job should be stated in terms of tasks rather than physical attributes.

> *Physical and mental attributes, and skills based on them (like lifting, driving, and reading) should be avoided to the greatest extent possible in the list of essential functions of the job. If a physical attribute seems unavoidable to perform the job, accompany that attribute with a description of the task or goal intended to be accomplished.*
>
> —Childcare Law Center

An infant teacher must be able to effectively diaper a child. In the event of a fire, teachers must be able to respond immediately to the emergency and evacuate children from the building. Both being able to diaper a child and assist in an emergency situation are essential functions of the job.

Job Interviews with Skill Demonstrations

Diapering a baby appropriately is an essential function of an infant teacher's job. This skill is different from the teacher's physical attribute of being able to lift 20 pounds.

> The new ADAAA expands the list of major life functions to include:
>
> • Functioning of immune system
> • Normal cell growth
> • Digestive, bowel, bladder
> • Neurological
> • Brain
> • Respiratory
> • Circulatory
> • Endocrine
> • Reproductive functions
> • Eating, sleeping, thinking, communicating, concentrating, lifting and bending

As part of the interview process, all candidates, including Jason, can be asked to demonstrate how they would diaper a baby. You, the employer, would provide a life-like doll for this part of the interview. In making this subtle shift from physical attribute to skill, leaders open the door wider to potentially qualified candidates.

The Visible Disability Exception

Applicants have the right to choose whether to disclose their disability. You, as a director, cannot ask an applicant if he or she has a disability. The same principle holds once you hire a person; the employee maintains the right to disclose his or her disability or not.

The one exception to this occurs when a clearly visible disability exists. Applicant Jason has one arm. You must treat Jason as you would treat all other applicants. However, when a disability is obvious, as in Jason's case, the "Visible Disability" exception may apply, according to Job Applications Network (JAN) attorney Linda Batiste. In that case, you can acknowledge the disability while asking Jason if he will be able to perform the functions of the job. To hear attorney Batiste's ADAAA podcast, go to http://www.jackstreet.com/jackstreet/WHRT.Batiste.cfm.

CHANGES TO THE AMERICANS WITH DISABILITIES ACT (ADA)

Let's put these new practices in context. The original ADA (see Appendix: Helpful Websites), enacted by Congress in 1990, supported employers' efforts to find the person best qualified for the job. The ADA also ensured that applicants with disabilities had equal access to employment and to maintaining their employment. The ADA did not require employers to favor an applicant with a disability over other, equally qualified applicants.

The ADA did require employers to make "reasonable accommodations" to allow qualified applicants to be interviewed, hired, and perform the job. Jason, for example, may request reasonable accommodations to be able to fully perform his duties if hired.

Case law, or decisions by judges who ruled on ADA lawsuits brought by either employers or applicants with disabilities, progressively cut back the reach of the ADA:

- In *Williams v. Toyota Motor Company,* the court held that plaintiff (a person with disabilities) must demonstrate an impairment that *substantially limits major life activity* in order to qualify for ADA protection (*Toyota Motor Manufacturing of Kentucky, Inc. v. Williams*, 2002).
- In *Sutton v. United Air Lines, Inc.*, 130 F.3d 893 (1999), the court held that a disability, if mitigated (made better) by medical treatment, no longer qualifies for ADA protection.

Congress, noting the intention of the ADA is to promote, not limit, equal opportunity for people with disabilities, took action to overturn these court decisions. The Amendments Act (ADAAA), effective January 1, 2009, overruled these Supreme Court decisions.

In addition to returning to the spirit of the law as intended (to give equal rights to those with disabilities), the ADA as amended has created and confirmed other employer responsibilities. Essential elements of the ADAAA include the following:

- The ADAAA protects a person with known physical or mental impairment that substantially limits one or more major life activities (NEW: functioning of immune system, normal cell growth, digestive, bowel, bladder, neurological, brain, respiratory, circulatory, endocrine and reproductive functions along with eating, sleeping, thinking, communicating, concentrating, lifting and bending).
- Impairments can be: physical (sight impaired, hearing impaired, wheel-chaired), conditions (epilepsy, diabetes, AIDS), or mental (bipolar, major depression, attention-deficit hyperactivity disorder), as well as record of impairment (cancer in remission), and/or Regarded as impaired.
- "Who is otherwise qualified for the job" means the person meets job requirements and is able to perform the functional requirements of the job with or without reasonable accommodations.
- "Reasonable accommodations" are adjustments or modifications to enable people with disabilities to enjoy equal employment opportunities (in applying for and performing on the job). Accommodations are individualized, tailored to fit the employee's needs.
- If an "undue hardship" would result from making a reasonable accommodation, the accommodation does not have to be made. Undue hardship includes excessive cost placing the organization in financial jeopardy.
- The "direct threat" exception comes about if an employee poses a significant risk of harm to him- or herself or others on the job that is likely to occur. Employers need not hire nor retain that employee.

Case Study: Disabilities and Reasonable Accommodations

Job applicant Selena, otherwise qualified to be a teacher's aide in your preschool program, tells you she is diabetic. To perform her job, Selena needs to test her blood sugar level at predictable intervals and ingest or inject insulin. She asks you to work with her to make "reasonable accommodations." What would you say?

Selena's potential employer must be ready to make reasonable accommodations to allow Selena to test and maintain her blood sugar levels. Making sure Selena has a safe storage location for her testing equipment and insulin, as well as adequate time to test and maintain her blood sugar, are both reasonable accommodations. If Selena and her physician state Selena needs a container of orange juice refrigerated nearby, her director will also reasonably accommodate this request. Administrators often worry about whether their budgets will cover the cost of making accommodations. Federal statistics show the average cost per accommodation is around $240; more than half are $500 or less.

The ADAAA requires employers to meet with the employee to discuss and together arrive at what reasonable accommodations will be made (*Cannice v. Northwest Bank*, 1999). When an applicant discloses her disability, she gives you permission to ask her what she needs to be able to perform the job if hired. Be sure to document this discussion. Listen to see if you can meet the applicant's needs without causing "undue hardship" to your program.

You can ask the applicant, if hired, to provide you with her doctor's assessment and description of the disability. This will help you be better informed. You can also ask for the doctor's recommendations for accommodations.

Utilizing that information from the doctor, sit down with the employee to discuss and coordinate necessary accommodations. Some employees may not feel they need accommodations. If the employer offers adequate accommodations and the employee rejects them, then the individual is no longer considered "a qualified individual with a disability" (ADAAA, 29 CFR Section 1630.9.).

ADAAA Exceptions to Making Reasonable Accommodations

Undue Hardship: In some cases, accommodations required for a potential employee with a disability are too costly for the program to bear. The ADAAA does not require an organization to endure an undue hardship, such as going into the red or out of business for the sake of one employee.

Direct Threat: In other cases, an applicant, even with the necessary accommodations, might still pose a *direct threat* to him- or herself or others. For example, an employee with chronic progressive multiple sclerosis who cannot hold a child without the strong possibility of dropping him or her poses a direct threat to his or her own and others' safety. Unless an applicant's seizure disorder can be controlled by medication, that applicant's clear possibility of having a seizure at work poses a direct threat. If either of these exceptions is present, undue hardship or direct threat, the well-being of the program outweighs the individual's needs.

By revising job descriptions to focus on tasks, administrators can prevent legal difficulties at job interviews. Interviews can be restructured from question-and-answer format to scenarios and demonstrations. In this way, applicants can share their own ways of meeting the essential functions of the job.

AWARENESS OF CULTURAL DIFFERENCES IN THE HIRING PROCESS

Hiring applicants of diverse ethnicities enhances program quality and breadth. Civil rights legislation requires employers to treat applicants of different national origins fairly (U.S. Dept. of Justice, 2000).

Case Study: Being Culturally Aware

Mei Wu applies to be a preschool lead teacher. Her credentials are stellar. At the interview, you ask Mei Wu to describe her strengths and accomplishments as a preschool teacher, and to explain why she is uniquely qualified to be a lead teacher. Mei Wu, flustered and embarrassed, is unable to answer the question satisfactorily.

Can we adapt our practices to accommodate cultural differences without subjecting ourselves to a lawsuit for discrimination? In Mei Wu's case, her Chinese heritage instills the practice of humility. In fact, her culture encourages emphasis on team accomplishments over individual recognition. With this cultural difference in mind, how might you revise the question you ask Mei Wu?

Focus the interview question to allow Mei Wu to answer the question without feeling she is betraying her cultural norms: "Could you describe some of your experiences as a preschool teacher that have prepared you to transition into the lead teacher position?" Or, "If I were to ask your employers about your strengths, what might they say?"

Given the requirement that all applicants must be asked the same set of questions, you need to document the changes you make to the questions along with your reason for doing so. In this case, the spirit rather than the letter of the law will lead to a fairer decision.

9 Supervision Challenges

Stepping Up to the Plate

Children depend on adults to do the right thing. Adults want to count on adults to do the right thing. When these expectations are not met, trouble brews for everyone. This chapter addresses legal challenges that result from supervising employees who are underperforming, resistant, or otherwise behaving inappropriately. In supervision, courage is the pathway to maintaining professionalism under interpersonal pressure.

FACING THE DISCOMFORT OF CONFRONTATION

Given the strong discomfort the majority of early childhood leaders have with confrontation—80%, in fact—supervision of difficult employees is problematic (Bruno, 2012). Inappropriate behavior is best dealt with in the moment, or soon thereafter.

Case Study: Managing a Resistant Employee

Toddler teacher Trina Marie resents having to create a classroom portfolio for accreditation purposes. After listening to her and other teachers' concerns, Director Stannah took steps to ease the process by providing time and professional support for portfolio development. Stannah has met repeatedly with Trina Marie, offering assistance while upholding the requirement. Trina Marie's section of the classroom portfolio is overdue by 2 weeks; her excuses are getting repetitive. What would you do if you were Stannah?

If we continually find excuses for an employee's unprofessional behavior or hope the employee will somehow improve, we take a serious risk. Similarly, waiting to confront a staff member until you have compiled a book listing her inappropriate actions, or until you have built up a full head of steam to at last take action, can put everyone in harm's way. How long do you wait before confronting teachers who arrive at work late, fail to create classroom portfolios, dismiss parents' concerns, lampoon every new idea at staff meetings, or stir up a swarm of gossip?

Everyone else in your program, from children to teachers to parents, watches you closely as their model. Your job is to give direct, honest, concise, and timely feedback.

To highlight the importance of that professional standard, let's look at the legalities of the following:

- Giving staff feedback on inappropriate behavior
- Probationary periods
- Employment "at will"
- Progressive discipline steps
- Replacing "progressive discipline" by returning to "employment at will"
- Grounds for immediate termination
- Confronting intangible behavior that is difficult to document (e.g., "attitude," other unprofessional behavior you have not personally witnessed)
- Setting gossip-free policies
- Complying with Americans with Disabilities Act as Amended (ADAAA) requirements on disciplinary action
- Addressing highly sensitive issues (e.g., body odor)
- Confidentiality requirements

Setting high standards for professional behavior without upholding those standards dumps you into a swamp of legal troubles.

What does it take to honor high standards, especially under pressure from within and without? The following practices, principles, policies, and forms will fuel your courage to take corrective action. Each time you take a stand for quality, you not only meet underlying legal requirements, you also lift your program's morale.

Giving Staff Feedback on Inappropriate Behavior

"If it isn't documented, it didn't happen," Head Start employees will tell you in a heartbeat, attesting to the importance of documenting inappropriate behaviors. This ensures a more accurate portrayal of the behavior and protection if a lawsuit arises. When you observe a staff member doing the wrong thing, take these steps to effectively address and document the behavior:

- Bring the inappropriate behavior to the employee's attention.
- Identify alternative, appropriate behaviors.

- Openly discuss the issues contributing to the behavior in order to arrive at a solution.
- Make a plan for changing the behavior from inappropriate to appropriate.
- Document the event and the discussion.

When you feel at odds about what is right, look to written standards and your own hard-earned experience with making difficult decisions. Guidelines to rely upon include the following:

- "Above all, we do not harm children," NAEYC's core value (NAEYC, 2005)
- Respect for children, families, peers, the program, the profession, and ourselves
- Your policies, procedures, and practices, along with your professional Code of Ethical Responsibility

Chapters 1 and 2 offer in-depth help in identifying the right thing to do. In the end, you have to take action sooner rather than later. Do the best you can, have a rational basis for your action, step up, document, and move on. Another prickly decision is waiting on your doorstep.

Picture yourself as if you were an athlete. When you begin your workout routine, you may have to drag yourself to the gym. While working out, you may feel as if your legs are made of lead and your arms are made of Jell-O™. However, with each workout you complete, you render the whole process of getting fit easier. Finally, working out becomes a healthy habit, perhaps not your favorite activity, but one you value.

So too with confronting employees: at first you may feel awkward, unfit, or perhaps as resistant as they are. Each time you step up to the challenge, you strengthen your skill and confidence. In the end, trust yourself to do the right thing. Confrontation may never be your preferred approach; however, you can look back and say, "I did it before and I can do it now." Most seasoned leaders agree that the value of confrontation far outweighs the discomfort.

The good news according to adult brain research is that as we mature, the brain's decision-making pathways become streamlined. In other words, we worry less, and make confident decisions more (Cozolino, 2006). On the flip side, however, we are neurologically hardwired to react defensively under threat; the amygdala's triggering of adrenalin or cortisol can wash away our clarity of purpose (Goleman, 2011). Consistently following and enforcing program policy and procedures can countermand that wash-out.

Documenting the Feedback Process

Feedback to employees about their performance is not an annual task—ideally, it is part of your daily routine. By providing and documenting your everyday comments to staff, you make the annual evaluation process easier: there will be no surprises. Effective feedback consists of the following components:

What: Are the specific facts about the behavior? What performance standard was violated?

When: Did the incident occur?

Who: Are the persons involved?

Where: Under what conditions did the event take place?

Why: Is this behavior happening?

How: What steps will be taken to turn inappropriate behavior into professional action? How is program quality affected?

Consider how you would apply this standard for feedback when meeting with Trina Marie, in the chapter case study, about her overdue portfolio:

- **What**: The classroom portfolio, required for accreditation, has not been turned in.
- **When**: The deadline was 2 weeks ago on (remind her of the due date).
- **Who**: Trina Marie is responsible for her section of the classroom portfolio.
- **Where**: Portfolios are due at your office.
- **Why**: Documenting each child's progress helps the child and family, and serves as a measure of teaching effectiveness; without classroom portfolios, the accreditation process fails.
- **How:** The portfolio is due Monday morning (date) at 6:30 a.m.; consultant Gracia is available for portfolio support; I will check in with you Wednesday and Friday to see how you are progressing; if the portfolio is not submitted Monday at 6:30, we will begin the first step of our program's Progressive Discipline process.

A sage legal adage, *res ipse loquitor* (the facts speak for themselves), sums the process up: feedback to employees needs to be simple, direct, factual, and timely. The facts you provide will speak for themselves. If a teacher is late, tell her the dates she was late and the times she arrived. Your documentation with "just the facts" will be powerful.

Your job is to make sure children and families receive the best possible care and education. Staff members need to model how to take responsibility for their own actions and how to learn and improve. If you avoid confronting the staff member, your inaction implies that the standards are lowered. Teachers who are doing their jobs well will begin to feel undervalued. Why should they work so hard when others with substandard performance face no consequences?

THE PROBATIONARY PERIOD

When you hire a new employee, set an amount of time for the probationary period during which you can terminate her employment "at will," or without cause. This probationary period usually lasts for 30 to 90 days. Union agreements, of course, may specify the length of this period.

During the employee's probation, observe and assess her performance. If, in your professional opinion, you think she is not the employee you need, you can terminate her without giving a reason. Simply say, "It's just not working out."

If you have followed best practices as a supervisor, you have documented your observations and have shared your concerns as they have arisen with the new employee. However, you are under no legal obligation to explain why you are letting her go. During the probationary period, "cause" is not required.

Once the initial probationary period has elapsed, your Progressive Discipline policy takes effect. With its "three-strikes-and-you're-out" procedures, progressive discipline requires you to complete a longer process to terminate the employee. As the second step of the progressive discipline procedure, an employee again may be put on probation. She gets to this point, however, only after other required actions have taken place. During the initial probationary period, the heavy machinery of progressive discipline is not evoked.

> Employers must be careful not to create an implied agreement during the probationary period. Employers should:
>
> - Avoid implied agreements through verbal assurances of continued employment.
> - Document any problems that arise during the period and retain evidence to refute claims of termination for illegal reasons.
> - Treat all employees consistently.
> - Understand improper grounds for termination, such as discrimination.
>
> *(Bruce, 2011, March 28)*

Seasoned directors offer commonsense advice: "If my gut tells me the new hire isn't a good fit, I have learned to trust my gut and let her go." Others say, "In hindsight, I wish I had terminated that employee during probation. I thought I could save her. I invested so much time in supervising her that I could have devoted to the children and other teachers." By using the phrase, "It's just not working out," you save yourself and your program a lot of aggravation.

Civil rights standards apply at any point from the hiring process through termination. Assess your intention. If a new hire is terminated because she is perceived as being too old or "doesn't fit in" due to her ethnicity or disability, that employee's rights are violated. The probationary period allows supervisors to terminate a person because she is not going to be able to do the job, not because of her status or identity (Cornell University Law School, 2012).

EMPLOYMENT "AT WILL"

"At will" status is just what it sounds like:

- *Employees are free to resign* at any time without explanation, depending on the employee's will.
- You, as an "at-will" *employer can terminate any employee* at any time without cause.

"At-will" employment has long been the standard in most states. Only Montana has modified the "at-will" policy with the Wrongful Discharge from Employment Act (WDEA). In Montana, firing an employee is unlawful if done for the following reasons:

1. Employee refuses to violate public policy or for reporting a violation of public policy;
2. There was no good cause and the probationary period has already passed;
3. The employer violates her own personnel policy. (Montana Code, 2008)

Every other state allows "at-will" policies with exceptions. Check your state law to see which, if any, exceptions your state mandates.

The important question about "at-will" is: "What does it mean to me and our program?" The answer is: "Very little, if you have a progressive discipline policy." Progressive discipline trumps "at-will" status.

In everyday terms, if your policies promise employees the opportunity to rectify their performance via a three-step process (written warning, probation, and termination), you must honor that policy. You are no longer free to tell an employee, "It's just not working out," as you would if "at-will" were your policy.

Here's an everyday analogy that may help you picture the legal effect of having progressive discipline policies on "at-will" status:

> A couple may be seriously romantically involved with one another. However, at any point, one person can walk away, leaving behind the relationship at will. In most cases, unless they have shared property, each person is free to leave the relationship. Once the couple marries, however, they make a contract with the state confirming their commitment legally. Now if one person wants to call it quits, she has to go through the steps of legally getting a divorce. Without the legal obligation, coming and going in relationships is freer.

Here's an early childhood analogy:

> Assume your state licensing policy does not set a minimum age for a person to be on the Authorized List for picking up a child (Chapter 3). Your program policy, however, requires people on the Authorized List to be 18 years of age or older. Your more rigorous policy replaces the state's policy. You cannot accept a 12-year-old on the Authorized List. Courts usually uphold policies that set a higher standard for quality.

Most early childhood programs use progressive discipline. Check your policies to determine your process for dealing with a staff member who is not performing. Progressive discipline, unlike "at-will" status, ensures an employee has the right to get help to improve her performance. If progressive discipline is your policy, you must follow it unless the employee's behavior is so egregious, such as drinking on the job, that you can terminate the employee immediately.

Courts have set two important standards for progressive discipline employers. You must:

- make a *conscientious rescue effort* to help the employee improve, and
- devote more time and attention to counseling the employee through *enhanced supervision*.

The consequence of both of these standards is that you, the employer, must take extra steps to help the employee turn things around. Notice how different this is from the simplicity of saying, "You're fired." Later, we'll look at what to do if you choose to reinstate "at-will" status.

PROGRESSIVE DISCIPLINE STEPS

"Three strikes and you're out" is the simplest way to describe the progressive discipline process. A baseball player steps up to bat to hit the ball and get on base. Similarly, the employee steps up to bat and wants to do well enough to get out of hot water.

The pitcher throws the first ball. If the baseball player hits the ball, she moves on and no longer fears striking out. If the player swings at the ball and misses, that's strike one. She has two more chances before she's out.

The employee who has been notified of her poor performance similarly steps up to the plate. If she does what is needed to improve her performance and she hits the first (written warning) or second ball (probation), she moves on toward earning a run with her performance.

The challenge comes when the employee fails to step up and hit any pitches. She is given two chances to improve; otherwise on her next violation, she strikes out.

Progressive Discipline Steps:

1. Written warning
2. Probation
3. Termination

Throughout the process, you are similar to the player's no-nonsense coach, assisting your employee in improving her performance. If she fails to improve, however, she is off the team. Children deserve our best performers.

Verbal Versus Written Warning

In some cases, the first step of progressive discipline is called "verbal warning" rather than "written warning." Given the need to document observations and actions in writing, verbal warnings are all but nonexistent. In reality, we can give numerous "verbal warnings" (which we document) before we initiate the formal progressive discipline steps (McDaniel, 2007).

Stannah, the director in the chapter case study, talked with Trina Marie on many occasions, listening to her concerns, offering assistance on creating her classroom portfolio, and essentially "warning" Trina Marie that the portfolio is required. This stage of supervision is also called "reflective supervision," wherein the supervisor helps the teacher to reflect on and improve her performance. Actions taken by the supervisor during reflective supervision are documented.

Reflective Versus Directive Supervision

At some point, the supervision process escalates from encouraging reflection to requiring direction. In reflective supervision, the supervisor assumes the employee wants to change her behavior.

In directive supervision, the employer acknowledges the employee's behavior isn't likely to change unless stronger action is taken. When progressive discipline is invoked, the supervisor must tell the employee that disciplinary action is being taken.

Step One: Written Warning

Regardless of whether the warning is verbal or written, the first progressive discipline step is identifying the staff member's inappropriate behavior and informing her of what is expected. Offer enhanced supervision to support the employee's improvement. Set a date (usually 1 week later) to evaluate whether the employee has met the standard. Inform the employee that if she fails to improve her performance, she will be placed on probation (Step Two of the progressive discipline process).

Director Stannah completes the first step of progressive discipline with teacher Trina Marie by:

- telling her that failing to turn in her classroom portfolio on time is unacceptable;
- stating the portfolio must be submitted by _____ (new date);
- asking her what action she will take to complete the portfolio by that date;
- establishing a plan of action describing what Trina Marie will do and what assistance Stannah will offer (set a date for your follow-up meeting); and
- advising her that failure to meet this requirement will result in her being placed on probation.

This process affords Trina Marie ample due process to know what she needs to change, to share her side of the story, and to make a plan for change.

Using and Signing the Corrective Action Form. Supervisors often use a Corrective Action form, asking the employee to sign the form and write her comments.

EMPLOYEE IMPROVEMENT PLAN OF ACTION

Employee's name: _____ Date and time: _____

Present at meeting: _____ (Names and job titles)

Director's concern: _____

_____ (Briefly and factually, identify incident and/or observation).

Expected behavior: _____

(Attach/refer to center policy, job description, program mission, licensing/accreditation standard, code of ethical behavior, etc.).

Plan for correcting problem: _____

_____

Follow-up meeting set for _____ (Date and time).

Employee will: _____

_____

Director/supervisor will: _____

_____

_____

Consequence if problem behavior is not corrected: _____

_____

Signatures of those present:
Employer: _____
Employee: _____
Witness (Name and title): _____
Employee's comments (Optional): _____
_____
_____
_____

On occasion, an angry employee may refuse to sign the form. In that case, show her the optional Employee Comments section on the form. Tell her she can explain her view of events there. Even if she refuses to sign the sheet, she documents her presence at the meeting.

Step Two: Probation

If the employee again fails to meet her agreed-upon obligation, she is placed on probation, the second step of progressive discipline. Because supervisors need to "make a conscientious rescue effort" to help the employee improve, the employee will be given one more chance before she strikes out. Because reaching Step Two is more serious than Step One, the consequence of failing to correct the problem is also more serious. At the end of the Step Two meeting, the supervisor must tell the employee that termination is the consequence of failure to meet the requirement. At this point, Trina Marie knows she either gets the task done or her job is over.

Step Three: Termination

Step three is termination. The employee has been given at least two opportunities, with support, to turn her behavior around. If she fails to meet the requirement, she decides her own fate. Step Three meetings are brief and no-nonsense. Stannah tells Trina Marie, "Because you have not completed your classroom portfolio as required, your work here is over."

Keep the drama to a minimum. Give the employee a reasonable, but brief, amount of time to pack up and depart. Tell her when she can expect to receive the last paycheck. Inform others only that the teacher is no longer with the program. The reasons are confidential. Have a plan to help children, families, and other staff adapt to the change.

If possible, include a third person at each of the disciplinary meetings. The person should be professional, respected, and objective. Her job is to witness the meetings. This third person's presence also diffuses the intensity of the one-on-one energy between you and the staff member. The witness signs the Corrective Action form, signifying her presence. She can be called upon later if the meetings are challenged in any way.

RETURNING TO EMPLOYMENT "AT WILL"

A small but compelling movement is growing among early childhood leaders to replace progressive discipline with the simpler "at-will" standard.

One director, Joyce from Massachusetts, had several grueling experiences with the progressive discipline process. Some employees had rectified one behavior at the last minute, only to engage in a different misbehavior. Joyce had devoted so much energy to progressive discipline with its required documentation and increased supervision that she often sacrificed time for other important tasks (D'Cruz, n.d.).

Joyce felt early childhood professionals should always do their best. She was willing to help employees improve their performance. However, she no longer wanted to be tied to progressive discipline as the way to ensure professionalism. Joyce painstakingly worked with an attorney for months, while using due process to discuss the possible policy change with her staff.

Everyone had ample opportunity to explore the benefits and detriments of both approaches, progressive discipline and "at will." Because Joyce's employees were not part of a union, she did not have to work with a union to make this change.

THINK ABOUT IT

How do you feel about progressive discipline? Are you interested in replacing progressive discipline with "at-will" employment? If so, where would you begin?

Ultimately, Joyce's program replaced the progressive discipline policy with the "at-will" standard. Employees retained the right to resign at will; the employer returned to the right to terminate an employee at will.

"AT-WILL" POLICY STATEMENT

Employment at _____ (Program's name) is "at will."

• Employees may resign at any time without stating the reason; and,
• The director can terminate an employee without cause at any time.

Employees are expected to perform at their professional best each day. Effective _____ (date), this policy replaces and nullifies all prior Progressive Discipline policies, written or oral (2 Cal. Transactions Forms, Bus. Tran, Sec. 12:60).

Some leaders feel progressive discipline ensures essential employee rights. Without progressive discipline, they maintain, employees would be taxed by fear and anxiety about losing their jobs. Other leaders say, "Great idea! All my teachers want to do their best. They know I support them in meeting their goals. Let's simplify our policies."

If you transition from progressive discipline to an "at-will" policy, be sure to provide ample time for everyone affected to discuss and give you feedback about the change. Work with an attorney to ensure all issues are adequately covered.

GROUNDS FOR IMMEDIATE TERMINATION

If you see a teacher threaten to slap a child, you would immediately want to protect the child and fire the employee. Similarly, if an employee smoked on the playground, you would terminate her. What other actions are so unacceptable that you would fire an employee on the spot? In most cases, any action that would cause harm or break the law is grounds for immediate termination.

THINK ABOUT IT

Have you encountered a situation that called for the immediate termination of an employee? What actions in the early childhood field do you think would be grounds for immediately firing an employee?

Courts have upheld the following causes for immediate termination:

- Violence
- Stealing
- Use of drugs or alcohol on the job
- Threatening a child or adult
- Violation of the law
- Refusal to participate in a police investigation

In each of these cases, the seriousness of the act suspends the otherwise required use of the progressive discipline process.

When the well-being of a child or an adult is threatened, and if a situation is dangerous or potentially dangerous, we must take action. In many cases, we must report the violation to the police and other state authorities such as licensing. In all cases, we need to document the incident.

Although we need to protect the confidentiality of the people involved, we also need to make sure no one is put in harm's way again. If the employee's action is so heinous that the police are involved, the employee's privacy is no longer protected. The police report makes the event public record. Every state has a Freedom of Information Act (FOIA), specifying that police records, as government agency records, are accessible to the public either free or for a nominal cost.

CONFRONTING DIFFICULT-TO-DOCUMENT BEHAVIOR

Facts are easier to document than intangibles. If you can measure a behavior objectively, you can document it. Documented, concrete, specific facts are compellingly persuasive. If an employee, whose workday begins at 6:30 a.m., arrives Monday at 7:00 a.m., Tuesday at 7:40, and Wednesday at 8:00, the facts will speak for themselves. The behavior is measurable by consulting the employee's time clock record.

Other behaviors, such as hearsay, are more difficult to prove. The Federal Rules of Evidence define *hearsay* as "a statement, other than one made by the declarant while testifying at the trial or a hearing, offered in evidence to prove the truth of the matter asserted" (Fed. R. Evidence 801[c]). Each state has its own definition of hearsay. Overall, these federal and state definitions of hearsay add up to indirect information about an event that was not witnessed directly.

Through the grapevine, you may hear that teachers are gossiping about families, each other, or you. Imagine calling the gossiper into your office to discuss the behavior but she responds with outrage.

Or, you hear that a substitute teacher is text messaging on the playground. When you monitor her, you instead observe the substitute earnestly engaging with the children. The rumor was not true, or at least not true for today.

If hearsay is difficult to document, intangible behavior such as "attitude" is even trickier to document and confront. "Attitude" evidenced by rolling the eyes, smirking, or giving a disgusted glare is not easy to document. Regardless of the difficulty in documenting these behaviors, you need to address them. Negativity, gossip, and insubordination sabotage program morale and undermine children's learning.

You have three choices about how to confront inappropriate behavior that is difficult to prove through documentation:

- Say, "It has come to my attention that _____." Do not say, "People are saying that _____." State the problem and identify the alternative, desired behavior.
- Use the "in-the-bushes" approach. If observing the inappropriate behavior is a challenge, situate yourself in a place where you are almost assured of witnessing the behavior. One director in New Jersey waited until the spring produced a thickly blooming forsythia bush and stepped out from behind the bush as soon as she personally heard the teacher's inappropriate remarks.
- Document "attitude" by factually describing your observations: for example, Trina Marie crossed her arms, rolled her eyes, and refused to contribute any ideas when each teacher was asked at the (date) staff meeting to identify one step he or she could take to progress on classroom portfolios.

Letting poor performance slide because the behavior is hard to document or confront is not an option. Document to the best of your ability and accept your responsibility for the sake of the children, families, and other employees who depend on you. Options a, b, and c in the quiz are appropriate; option d is not.

QUIZ

Trina Marie not only drags her feet on completing her classroom portfolio, she also gossips to every other teacher about the ridiculousness of the portfolio requirement. Trina Marie encourages teachers to resist doing the portfolios or to do them in a shoddy manner. Other teachers complain to you about this. No one, however, has the courage to confront Trina Marie. What would you do?

a. Coach teachers individually on how to confront a gossiper.
b. Provide staff training on ways to stop gossip, especially for teachers who are afraid of conflict.
c. Pop into the staff lounge when you know Trina Marie will be there, call her into your office, and say, "People are complaining that you are gossiping about not doing classroom portfolios."
d. Give up on changing Trina Marie's behavior. After all, she is good with the children.

Setting Gossip-Free Policies

Gossip is a destructive force in organizations. Gossip, or talking about another person who is not present with the intention to harm that person's reputation, turns a professional environment into a land mine.

Gossip is:

- Talking about another person who is not present,
- With the intention of harming that person's reputation;
- Listening to gossip is gossiping.

—Bruno, 2012

Gossiping is different from free speech. Gossip is, by definition, done with the intention to harm another person's reputation. When behavior becomes destructive, that behavior needs to be confronted. Unless gossip is about a matter of public concern, it is not likely to be protected by the First Amendment. For example, if an employee's gossip amounts to "whistle blowing" on the misdeeds of an organization, those statements may be protected (West Virginia Employment Law Letter, 2008).

Some labor lawyers argue that employees have the right to state their opinion of their boss or other employees. You might want to consult with a lawyer knowledgeable about labor law before you institute a "No Gossip" policy. If you decide that gossip is inappropriate in a professional work setting, consider taking these steps:

- Add to your job descriptions: "Will maintain a gossip-free work environment."
- Give employees notice that gossiping is inappropriate and will be confronted.
- Provide training for staff that includes "gossip stoppers" for peers—statements teachers can use to step out of gossip's way without being shunned.
- Invite employees to review and sign an Agreement to Resolve Issues policy.
- Hold gossipers accountable by taking them through the progressive discipline process, as for any other infraction.

THINK ABOUT IT

Before taking corrective action, check your motivation and beliefs: Do you think gossip is acceptable in the workplace? Is gossip an unchangeable dynamic of "it is what it is" that we must accept? Do you find the occasional bit of juicy gossip irresistible? Do you think you would be effective in establishing a gossip-free work environment?

Some organizational behaviorists maintain that gossip is a useful dynamic. It provides the leader with knowledge about influential employees and underlying office gripes. Decide what is important to you.

Teachers report that they fear standing up to a gossiper. If a teacher doesn't go along with a gossiper, the teacher puts herself in danger of being mocked or shunned. The following "gossip stoppers" can be used effectively by peers to stop gossip while allowing them to step out of harm's way:

- I need to focus on the children now.
- Would you be willing to talk with the person you are having trouble with?
- Talk with the director; she'll help you resolve this.
- I am not comfortable talking about a person who is not present.
- I promised myself I wouldn't gossip.
- Because I can't help you with that problem, please don't bring it to me again.

Armed with these simple and honest statements, teachers can get back to business and not get ground up in the gossip mill.

An employee who is the target of gossipers may decide to sue the gossipers individually for "defamation of character." Defamation is either libel or slander. Slander is spoken, oral, nonpublished words. Libel is written, broadcast, or published words. Gossip is more likely to qualify as slander. The elements of defamation are:

1. a defamatory statement,
2. published to third parties (orally is slander; written or broadcast is libel),
3. which the speaker knew to be false.

The statement must be false for the speaker to be liable. It must also be believable. Public figures such as politicians and movie stars may be exempt from protection.

Agreement to Resolve Problems

You might also invite teachers to sign a problem-solving agreement. Once employees have discussed and signed this agreement, place it in their files. Use the document in follow-up disciplinary discussions if gossip, rather than problem solving, erupts.

PROBLEM-SOLVING AGREEMENT

I, _____, an employee of _____, agree to promptly and directly raise any issue I have with another staff member. I agree to work with my colleague to find a mutually agreeable solution, building on both of our strengths. If, after a good-faith effort, the conflict remains unresolved, I will request a meeting with my director (or designee) and my colleague. I agree to take to that meeting at least two possible solutions that will honor the organization's and both persons' needs. I agree neither to gossip about, nor hold back from, resolving an issue that affects the quality of care and education. I will participate fully in staff development sessions on problem-solving techniques.

_____ (Signature) _____ (Date)

You can also remind employees of the requirement in the NAEYC Code of Ethical Conduct (2005):

> When we have concerns about the professional behavior of a co-worker, we shall first let that person know of our concern in a way that shows respect for personal dignity and for the diversity to be found among staff members, and then attempt to resolve the matter collegially and in a confidential manner. (p. 5)

Coupling this professional standard with your own antigossip policies gives you ample back-up in upholding a gossip-free work environment (Bruno, 2012).

COMPLYING WITH ADAAA REQUIREMENTS ON DISCIPLINARY ACTION

As discussed in Chapter 8, the Americans with Disabilities Act as Amended (2009) assures employees equal opportunity to apply for, be hired, and enjoy the benefits of being on the job. The ADAAA does not entitle an employee to be held to a lower standard for professional performance. The purpose of reasonable accommodations is to help an employee perform the essential functions of the job. If an employee fails to do his or her job, whether that employee is disabled or not, the employee will be held accountable, just as any other employee would be.

Case Study: Disciplinary Action and Disability

Infant teacher Tarissa for years was a model employee, attentive to children and their families and an energetic team member. Over the last 3 months, Tarissa has been moody, late for work, late with her paperwork, uncaring about parents' concerns, and whining. Last week, you saw Tarissa walking hand in hand into a bar with a man you had never seen before. Today, a parent tells you she doesn't trust Tarissa with her child any longer. What do you do?

The ADA applies only if the employee discloses her disability. Just as in the hiring process, you, the employer, cannot ask an employee if she is disabled. An employee who discloses her disability, however, places herself under the protections of the ADA. What would you do as the director in Tarissa's case?

Tarissa's lateness, inadequate paperwork, inattention to parents, and nonstop whining must each be confronted. When you call her in, you can address one issue at a time, giving her the facts, and reminding her of what is expected.

You may also want to ask her: "Is there anything you'd like to share with me, Tarissa? Your performance since March has been very different from your overall performance here. I am concerned." If she ignores you, continue to hold her to a professional standard through reflective and/or directive supervision as needed.

If she breaks down crying and tells you her husband deserted her for his younger secretary, she can't seem to concentrate, and her doctor tells her she is depressed, she opens the door to possible ADA assistance.

Chronic depression is likely to be covered by the ADA (Bruno & Batiste, 2010). However, in *Maslanka v. Johnson & Johnson, Inc.*, the court ruled that depression and anxiety were not protected under the ADA because they did not rise to the level of a disability under the ADA. Thus, if depression does rise to a chronic level, it would be protected (Onder, 2009).

Because Tarissa has disclosed her disability and that disability appears to "rise to the level" of ADA protection, you can ask her for:

- her doctor's description of the disability and how the disability is treated, and
- the doctor's recommendations for reasonable accommodations so Tarissa can restore her ability to perform at a professional level in the workplace.

You cannot ask an employee such as Tarissa if she has a disability, even if you suspect she does. The employee is not obligated to tell you about her disability. She has the choice to disclose it or not.

Aided by the doctor's recommendations and your new knowledge about Tarissa's disability, you and she can discuss what she needs to perform her job at a professional level.

The accommodation may be as simple as storing her medication in a private location and covering her break while she takes the medication. As long as the accommodation is reasonable, doable, and makes it possible for the employee to do her job, all is well. Keep the reasonable accommodation process confidential and document it adequately.

Case Study: Addressing Highly Sensitive Issues

Toddler teacher Gertrude's body odor has become so offensive that parents take their questions to her team teacher, children squeeze their noses and refuse to sit on her lap, and teachers throw the windows open at staff meetings to lessen the smell. Gertrude's lesson plans are brilliant, she trolls second-hand stores for creative supplies for class activities, and she is always willing to take on whatever you assign to her.

Gertrude is a private person, difficult to approach on anything personal. How do you deal with this supervision challenge? Begin by asking yourself: "Is Gertrude performing the essential functions of her job?" If "building partnerships with families" and "engaging directly with the children at their level" are part of her job description, the answer is no. You have to take action, regardless of how uncomfortable you are with discussing body odor.

Present the employee with the facts. Describe the problem and the desired change. For example, "Gertrude, the strong odor from your midsection is causing children and families to avoid you, and your team teacher appears overwhelmed with responsibility. What can you do, or how can I help you, eliminate this barrier to your doing your job?" Unless Gertrude discloses a disability that causes the body odor, proceed as you would with any other issue. Help her remedy the problem so she can do her best with children and families.

Gertrude may surprise you by confiding, "I didn't want to mention this because I am so embarrassed. As a result of unexpected surgery I had over the summer, I now have a colostomy bag. I don't know how to deal with it!"

Gertrude may have revealed a disability. With the amendments to the ADA, the following major bodily functions are covered: endocrine and bowel functions. Thanks to your sensitive and honest conversation with Gertrude, a door is now open for you to ask for the doctor's description of the disability and recommendations for reasonable accommodations.

If the cause of the odor is personal preference, the protections of the ADA do not apply. Perhaps one staff member refuses to use deodorant because of its chemicals. Another staff member is used to bathing once a week only. Or, a teacher from a different ethnic background uses pungent spices that cause her skin to smell strongly. In these cases, you need to weigh the individual's preference or practice with the needs of the overall program and take action accordingly.

For assistance, look back to our discussion in Chapter 6 on legalities that arise when majority and minority rights conflict.

CONFIDENTIALITY REQUIREMENTS

At work, employees' individual records are confidential. The employee has a right to see her file, even though she cannot remove the file from your office. Nor can she add or subtract anything from the file without your authorization.

You have the responsibility to maintain an accurate, up-to-date, confidential file on each employee. Beyond that, absent a legal investigation where the data in the file is subpoenaed, the employee's privacy is to be maintained.

Maintaining confidentiality of an individual's work history and records, including evaluations, disciplinary action, and honors and awards, is a simple matter unless something extraordinary happens.

Some information, such as name, title, and rate of pay, in an employee file may be shared with the public if the employer is a government agency or if the organization is carrying out government work. However, private companies may create their own confidentiality policies.

Employee health records are protected as confidential by the Health Insurance Portability and Accountability Act of 1996 (HIPAA). Employers who have group health plans or who have any health-related information in files must keep that information confidential. This may include requests for time off that describe a medical condition. Because supervisors often need to see an employee's file, anything with medical information on it should be kept in a separate file (Guerin & DelPo, n.d.).

Teacher Terrence may quit suddenly to return to Nigeria to help his ailing father. Unless Terrence authorizes you to share the reason for his departure with others, you are obliged to keep this confidential. If people inquire as to Terrence's well-being, you can provide only the information on how to reach Terrence that he has authorized you to give. Similarly, if a staff member is in the hospital, unless she authorizes it, you cannot tell others the reason for the hospitalization. The fact that she is hospitalized is public record, however, unless she tells the hospital not to disclose this information (HIPPA World Privacy Forum, 2009).

Confidentiality as a principle and practice is rarely challenged. When out-of-the-ordinary events happen, however, you may have to remind people of your commitment to confidentiality. If you terminate an employee suddenly, other teachers, parents, and children will want to know why. You may find yourself being pressed to explain what happened. Don't. Instead, honestly tell people that you are bound by confidentiality standards to keep the matter private. Even if the terminated teacher tells everyone you treated her unfairly, you still must honor this standard. See Chapter 7 for additional information on this confidentiality requirement.

10 Insurance

Are You Fully Covered?

The fear of being sued is usually associated with owing hundreds of thousands of dollars. The only way to protect your center from having to pay money damages is to purchase insurance. Yes, we know that insurance is probably your least favorite topic in this book (that's why we put it at the end!). But, it's no less important than everything else. You may be thinking, "my center has insurance, so I can skip this chapter." However, unless you have spoken with your insurance agent recently and made a thorough review of all your insurance policies, it will be worth your while to pay attention.

The information about insurance in this chapter is essentially the same whether your program is for-profit, not-for-profit, Head Start, or a school-based program. The greater the number of children you care for, the more insurance you will need.

WHAT DOES INSURANCE PROTECT?

Despite your best efforts, there is no way to prevent all accidents and illnesses from occurring in your child care center. Therefore, you must rely on insurance. Insurance will shield your center from the following risks:

- *Financial damage*—A parent sues your program because her child became sick after eating lunch served in your center.
- *Legal expenses*—A parent accuses her child's teacher of child abuse and sues your center. Another teacher sues your program for wrongful termination, claiming she was fired because of her religion. You will need legal assistance to defend your center.
- *Medical expenses*—A child incurs $10,000 of emergency room medical bills after falling off the outdoor playground equipment.
- *Property damage*—Your building is damaged by fire and is closed for 2 months. The cost to make repairs and replace equipment is $100,000. Your lost income is $60,000.

The only way to protect your program from these risks is to have adequate liability insurance, workers' compensation insurance, property insurance, and commercial car insurance (if you own vehicles). Ask about a Business Owners Policy (BOP) that combines core insurance coverage offerings at a lower cost with fewer administrative challenges. Workers' compensation insurance protects employees who are injured on the job.

It's a hard truth that your center will probably be held liable for any injury suffered by a child while enrolled. Your center (not the parent or child) is responsible for the health and safety of the child. It won't matter who was at fault, or whether it was an accident that couldn't be prevented. Right or wrong, the parent can sue.

Therefore, you will want adequate insurance to protect your center from all of the risks associated with caring for children. Insurance companies will offer policies that offer different coverage and exclusions. Not all insurance policies are the same. Here are the key things to look for in insurance policies:

General Coverage

- General liability insurance that protects your operations
- Professional liability insurance that protects against wrongful acts (such as failure to properly supervise a child)
- Sexual/physical/child abuse coverage
- Directors' and officers' liability coverage (to defend against lawsuits against your board and officers)
- Data breach (coverage for someone hacking your computers and releasing names and Social Security numbers of the parents or staff)

Coverage for Employers: Losses for Employers Arising from Employees

- Employment practices liability coverage (to protect your program against claims made by employees: discrimination, wrongful termination, sexual harassment)
- Employee benefits liability coverage (if you offer employee benefits)
- Employee dishonesty (theft of money or property)

Coverage for Property

- Property insurance (coverage for your building, business personal property [toys, equipment, computers, desks, etc.], leasehold/tenant improvements made by *you*). You want replacement coverage for all of your playground equipment, computers, desks, toys, supplies, and so forth. For some centers this will amount to hundreds of thousands of dollars of coverage.

Coverage for Accidents and Medical Expenses

- Accidental medical expense coverage
- You want a separate accident policy that will cover smaller claims. For larger claims, the general liability policy will apply. The accident policy should cover for medical expenses of at least $10,000. Note: in some parts of the country you may be able to get coverage limits up to $25,000. Although this will cost more, it may be well worth it, considering the tendency for parents to sue for damages. You want this separate accident policy to reduce the number of claims made against your general liability policy. (This will keep your liability policy premiums stable.) Ideally, you want your accident policy to be "primary." That is, it will cover the claim before the parent has to make a claim against his or her own policy. Primary coverage may not always be available.

Other Coverage

- Legal defense costs (This should be unlimited; you don't want any legal fees to reduce the amount of your liability coverage. These costs will be expressed as defense costs "outside the limits.")
- Business income and extra expense (This is coverage for loss of income on a short-term basis, rent, and other expenses if your center has to temporarily close because of fire, hail damage, etc.)
- Umbrella liability (This increases coverage amounts for general and professional insurance, sexual abuse, workers' compensation, vehicle, and employee benefit coverage. You want at least $1 million of umbrella coverage.)
- Additional insured (If your center leases space or you rent space for a graduation ceremony or special activity, you can add the

name of the landlord as an "additional insured" to protect the owner of the building from a lawsuit arising out of your program.)

- "Occurrence form" versus "claims made form" (Policies that are "occurrence form" will cover claims after the policy has expired or after the company has gone out of business as long as the incident occurred during the policy coverage dates. However, a "claims made" policy will cover only those claims made while your center is covered by the policy. Therefore, look for an "occurrence form" policy.)

Be sure to check that the company you choose is financially secure and has at least an "A" rating from the A. M. Best Company (see Appendix: Helpful Websites).

What's not covered by your insurance policy may be as important as what is covered. Ask to see exactly what is excluded from coverage in your policy. In general, unless there is specific coverage exclusion, your policy should protect you.

Be sure the exact legal name of your center is listed on your insurance policy: "Sunshine Enterprises, LLC Doing Business as the ABC Child Care Center." If you listed only Sunshine Enterprises and a parent sued the ABC Child Care Center, it's possible that your insurance would not cover you.

It's not necessary for your staff to have their own liability insurance because they are covered under your center's policy.

VEHICLE INSURANCE

Transporting children on field trips or taking them to and from your center creates a high degree of risk because of the possibility of multiple injuries and property damage. If your center owns vehicles that are used to transport children, you should have a least $1 million in liability insurance, in addition to physical damage coverage on the vehicles.

If your staff will ever use their own vehicles for business purposes, you should purchase "hired and non-owned" vehicle insurance. Your staff may use their own vehicles to pick up supplies, run errands, or transport a child. This insurance protects your center against a lawsuit by someone who was injured or whose property was damaged by the staff's vehicle. The insurance kicks in only when a claim is not covered by the staff's own vehicle insurance. Watch out for situations where staff are transporting children. Their personal vehicle insurance will likely not cover them, so any claim for injuries or damage are likely to fall on your center. If you are allowing staff to transport children, insist that their vehicle insurance cover them for this business use.

Staff are not covered by a "hired and non-owned" policy. Their own insurance is their sole protection. This is another reason to insist that staff be properly covered if they use their vehicle for business purposes. If a staff person is injured while driving his or her own vehicle, your workers' compensation policy should provide coverage. However, it's possible for a workers' compensation claim to be denied if the employee's vehicle insurance does not cover for the business use. Bottom line: if your employees are going to be using their vehicles for business purposes, it's in both your and your employees' interests to be sure that their vehicle insurance properly covers them for their business activities.

If staff members will occasionally (or regularly) use their vehicles for business purposes, check their driving records before hiring them. You can refuse to hire someone because of a poor driving record. Talk to your insurance agent about the consequences of hiring someone with a poor driving record. Your insurance company is likely to require you to obtain proof that the staff person has his or her own vehicle insurance. The staff person's vehicle insurance should offer coverage limits of $100,000 per person and $300,000 per accident. Never allow staff persons to use their own vehicles for business purposes until you have first discussed this with your own insurance agent.

VISITORS AND WORKERS ON YOUR PREMISES

It is likely that numerous people are on your premises in addition to your staff and families. This includes people who come to enhance your program: musician, aerobics instructor, Santa Claus, and so on. But it also includes others, such as your cleaning crew, snow removal company, plumber, handyperson, and so forth. You should require that all those who work on your property carry general liability insurance and have workers' compensation insurance coverage. If they don't, and are injured while on your premises, your center could be liable, and this can raise your insurance premiums. Ask to see a certificate of insurance and ask to be listed on their insurance policy as an additional insured.

DIRECTORS' AND OFFICERS' INSURANCE

When an unhappy parent or member of your staff decides to sue your center, he or she may also individually sue your board of directors. In addition, you may have lawsuits from your staff for discrimination, harassment, or wrongful termination. Lawsuits by parents could be for failure to keep their child safe, or for discrimination against them. Outside parties could also sue the board for mismanagement of the center's assets. To protect against these situations, your center should purchase directors' and officers' insurance. This insurance provides individual protection to board members against "wrongful acts" while making decisions as a board member. Because a board director can be held personally responsible for the decisions of your center, some persons may not agree to serve on your board without this insurance. Without it, board members would have to pay their own legal fees if sued. If you are an owner of a for-profit center, you should have your own business liability insurance. Ask your insurance agent about getting directors' and officers' insurance as well.

SHOPPING FOR INSURANCE AND AN INSURANCE AGENT

Because insurance policies can vary a lot, it's a good idea to shop around to find the best coverage for your program. Show your policy to other companies and ask them to compare their coverage and services. You should do comparisons with other policies at least every 3 to 5 years.

When shopping for insurance, you should also pay particular attention to choosing a good insurance agent. Look for a person with experience in insuring many child care centers. You want someone who understands the child care industry as well as someone who has experience and knowledge of the general insurance industry. For example, if you rent, you want your insurance agent to know that she should review your lease to see who is responsible for insuring any leasehold improvements made by you or the landlord.

A sign of a good insurance agent is someone who will work with you to identify safety issues (leaky roof, bad stairs, etc.) to reduce the risk of a claim. It's also a good sign if a representative of your insurance company visits your center. Follow the agent's advice about fixing potential hazards. Insurance agents have seen disasters happen at centers that did not correct such hazards. Talk to your insurance agent about the possibility of bringing in a risk management expert to help you reduce the risks of injury. If you follow the expert's advice it can help keep your premiums lower.

Does your agent return your calls promptly and is he or she willing to spend the necessary time to answer all of your questions? Ask for a copy of the claim form and learn how to fill it out. You should develop a close business relationship with your agent so he or she can advocate on your behalf with the insurance company when there is a claim.

Contact your insurance agent right away if:

- there is any injury to a child or staff person in your program;
- there is any change in your program (increase or decrease in the number of children or change in your hours, holidays open, extended hours, sleepover, etc.—such changes may be covered for no additional charge or for a small fee. You don't want to take the risk that you are not covered when such changes occur.)
- a parent threatens to sue your center; or
- your child care licensing agent cites your center for rule violations.

Your agent should be someone who welcomes your calls, works to help you reduce risks, and carefully explains how insurance can protect your program.

INSURANCE COVERAGE LIMITS

Your business liability policy will provide two types of coverage limits: "occurrence" and "aggregate." *The occurrence limit* is the amount of coverage you have for each incident, no matter how many children are injured. *The aggregate limit* is the amount of coverage you have for all claims paid under the policy, for the term of the policy (usually 1 year).

How much insurance coverage should you get? The simple answer is: as much as you can afford. A general rule with liability insurance is that you get what you pay for. Ideally, you will want $1 million occurrence and $1 to $3 million aggregate for both general liability coverage and professional liability coverage. If you have $500,000 of per-occurrence coverage, the cost of increasing this to $1 million is going to be much less than the cost of the first $500,000 of coverage. To cover claims above these amounts, purchase umbrella liability insurance. If you have multiple locations, be sure your aggregate limits apply per location.

For many child care programs, purchasing adequate insurance coverage can be expensive. Here are some ways to manage these costs:

- Conduct an annual review of all your insurance policies to see if you are under- or over insured.
- Raise the deductibles on your property and vehicle insurance policies. This will lower the premiums.

Although the cost of insurance may be burdensome, it's part of the cost of doing business. Do not rely on there being a perfect world: "It will never happen to me. My staff will never be dishonest. There will never be a case of child abuse in my center." Don't hesitate to get adequate coverage because you have never been sued in the past, or you've never had an accident up until now. It takes only one lawsuit to turn things upside down. Also, don't assume you are protected somehow from a lawsuit because your center has no money in the bank. A parent who wins a claim against you in court may be able to put a lien on your center's assets.

LIABILITY WAIVERS

Some child care centers try to reduce risks by having parents sign a liability waiver. Such a liability waiver might read, "By signing this statement, the parent agrees to hold the ABC Child Care Center harmless for any injuries suffered by their child while enrolled with this program." We do not recommend that you count on such liability waivers to protect you against a parent lawsuit for a number of reasons. Some states don't recognize such waivers. Unless your liability waiver has been carefully prepared by an attorney, any protection can be lost if it's poorly written. Any waiver will likely not protect you from an injured child who did not sign the statement from suing you later. Children may be able to sue up to age 18 or 21 for injuries suffered earlier in life. Talk to an attorney before trying to prepare a liability waiver.

Very few people enjoy spending time reviewing their insurance policies. But, it's essential to understand what type of insurance coverage you have to ensure you are properly protected. Finding and working with an experienced insurance agent who understands your business can make a big difference when someone files a claim against your center.

Helpful Websites

CHAPTER 1

- **Blink: Thin-Slicing Skills**
  http://www.gladwell.com/blink
- **Make Decisions**
  http://career.berkeley.edu/Plan/MakeDecisions.stm
- **Thought Awareness, Rational Thinking, and Positive Thinking**
  http://www.mindtools.com/pages/article/newTCS_06.htm

CHAPTER 2

- **American Civil Liberties Union**
  http://www.aclu.org
- **Lambda Legal**
  http://www.lambdalegal.org
- **National Association for the Advancement of Colored People**
  http://www.naacp.org
- **National Women's Law Center**
  http://www.nwlc.org
- **State Directory of Mandated Reporting Rules**
  http://tinyurl.com/2b4c78k

CHAPTER 3

- **State Child Care Center Regulations**
  http://www.nrckids.org/states
- **National Association for Regulatory Administration**
  http://www.naralicensing.org/Licensing_Study

CHAPTER 4

- **Council for Exceptional Children Publications for Families and Educators**
  http://www.cec.sped.org/Content/NavigationMenu
  AboutCEC/Communities/Families/CEC_Publications_and.
  htm
- **Early Childhood News: In Support of Family-Teacher Partnerships**
  http://www.earlychildhoodnews.com/earlychildhood/
  article_view.aspx?ArticleID=359
- **Family-Centered Practice**
  http://www.childwelfare.gov/famcentered
- **Harvard Family Research Project**
  http://www.hfrp.org
- **National Child Protective Seat Certification Course**
  http://cert.safekids.org
- **National Highway Traffic Safety Administration**
  http://www.nhtsa.gov/cps/cpsfitting/index.cfm
- **Partnering with Families and Communities**
  http://pdonline.ascd.org/pd_online/success_di/el200405_
  epstein.html
- **Recognizing Child Abuse and Neglect: Signs and Symptoms**
  http://www.childwelfare.gov/pubs/factsheets/signs.cfm
- **The United States of Education: The Changing Demographics of the United States and Their Schools**
  http://www.centerforpubliceducation.org/You-May-Also-Be-
  Interested-In-landing-page-level/Organizing-a-School-YMABI/
  The-United-States-of-education-The-changing-demographics-
  of-the-United-States-and-their-schools.html

CHAPTER 5

- **SIDS-Related Laws**
  http://www.ncsl.org/issues-research/health/sudden-infant-
  death-syndrome-laws.aspx

CHAPTER 6

- American Academy of Pediatrics
  http://www.aap.org
- Commonly Asked Questions About Child Care Centers and ADA
  http://www.ada.gov/childq&a.htm
- Council on Exceptional Children, Division of Early Childhood's Position Statement
  http://www.dec-sped.org/uploads/docs/about_dec/position_concept_papers/Position%20Statement_Cultural%20and%20Linguistic%20Diversity_updated_sept2010.pdf
- Discrimination Based on Sexual Orientation Prohibited
  http://www.irem.org/pdfs/publicpolicy/Anti-discrimination.pdf
- Federal Communications Commission
  http://www.fcc.org
- Head Start
  http://www.facebook.com/l/GAQH_m70w/eclkc.ohs.acf.hhs.gov/hslc/tta-system/cultural-linguistic
- Healthy Kids, Healthy Care: Parents as Partners in Promoting Healthy and Safe Child Care
  http://www.healthykids.us
- NAEYC's Position Statement on Cultural and Linguistic Responsiveness
  http://www.naeyc.org/positionstatements/linguistic
- National Dissemination Center for Children with Disabilities
  http://nichcy.org
- National Early Childhood Technical Assistance Center
  http://nedtac.org
- NCLB Action Briefs: Programs of English-Language Learners
  http://www.publiceducation.org/portals/nclb/lep/index.asp
- Nemeth's Assessment of Early Childhood Field
  http://www.languagecastle.com
- New Hampshire Department of Education
  http://www.education.nh.gov/instruction/integrated/esol/index.htm
- New Hampshire School System's Policies and Practices
  http://sprise.com/special.aspx?id=794
- The Public Education Network
  http://www.publiceducation.org/portals/nclb/lep/index.asp
- WIDA
  http://www.WIDA.us

CHAPTER 7

- **Able2Know**
  http://www.able2know.org/forum/parenting_and_childcare
- **About.com**
  http://www.tinyurl.com/4y5k4ft
- **Americans with Disabilities Act Home Page**
  http://www.usdoj.gov/crt/ada
- **Facebook, Daycare.com**
  http://www.daycare.com/forum
- **Google**
  http://www.google.com/alerts
- **Monitoring the Internet**
  http://www.reputation.com **and** http://www.socialmetrix.com
- **Parenting Forums**
  http://www.parentingforums.org/forum.php
- **Yellow Pages**
  http://www.yellowpages.com
- **Yelp**
  http://www.yelp.com

CHAPTER 8

- **Americans with Disabilities Act Home page**
  http://www.usdoj.gov/crt/ada
- **Interviewing for an ECE (Early Childhood Educator)**
  http://www.askanece.com/for-teachers/ece-job-interview-questions
- **JAN (Job Accommodation Network)**
  http://askjan.org
- **U.S. Equal Employment Opportunity Commission**
  http://www.eeoc.gov
- **Writing Effective Job Descriptions**
  http://www.sba.gov/content/writing-effective-job-descriptions

CHAPTER 9

- **Conflict Resolution and Negotiation Articles**
  http://www.abetterworkplace.com/conflicts.html

- **Corrective Action: Progressive Discipline**
  http://www.iu.edu~/uhrs/training/ca/progressive.html
- **Employment at Will: What Does It Mean?**
  http://www.nolo.com/legal-encyclopedia/employment-at-will-definition-30022.html
- **Freedom of Information Act (FOIA)**
  http://www.foia.gov
- **Problem-Solving Techniques**
  http://www.mindtools.com/pages/main/newMN_TMC.htm
- **Stop the Gossip, Save Your Career**
  http://career-advice.monster.com/in-the-office/workplace-issues/stop-the-gossip-save-your-career-hot-jobs/article.aspx

CHAPTER 10

- **First Children's Finance**
  http://www.firstchildrensfinance.org

References

CHAPTER I

Blackstone, W. (2003). Proceedings in equity. In T. M. Cooley (Ed.), *Commentaries on the laws of England: In four books* (3rd rev. ed.). Clark, NJ: The Lawbook Exchange.

Bruno, H. E. (2011, January). The neurobiology of emotional intelligence: Using your brain to stay cool under pressure. *Young Children*, 22–27.

Bruno, H. E. (2012b). *What you need to lead an early childhood program: Emotional intelligence in practice*. Washington, DC: NAEYC.

Buchanan, L., & O'Connell, A. (2006, Jan.). A brief history of decision making. *Harvard Business Review, 84*, 32–41.

Cozolino, L. (2006). *The neuroscience of human relationships: Attachment and the developing social brain*. New York: W. W. Norton & Company.

Cozolino, L. (2010). Three keys to understanding people who push your buttons. Radio interview. *Heart to heart conversations on leadership: Your guide to making a difference*. Retrieved from http://www.BAMradionetwork.com; http://www.hollyelissabruno.com

Dobbs, D. D. (1993). *Law of remedies hornbook* (2nd ed.). Eagan, MN: West Publishing Company.

Feeney, S., & Freeman, K. (2000). *Ethics and the early childhood educator: Using the NAEYC Code*. Washington, DC: National Association for the Education of Young Children.

Gilkey, R., Cacede, R., & Kilts, C. (2010). When emotional reasoning trumps IQ. *Harvard Business Review, 88*, 27. Retrieved from http:/hbr.org/2010/09/when-emotional-reasoning-trumps-IQ/ar/1

Gladwell, M. (2005). *Blink: The power of thinking without thinking* (2nd ed.). New York: Little, Brown & Company.

Goleman, D. (1995). *Emotional intelligence: Why it matters more than IQ*. New York: Bantam Books.

Goleman, D. (2006). *Social intelligence: The new science of human relationships*. New York: Bantam Dell.

Kerly, D. M. (1890). *Historical sketch of the equitable jurisdiction of the court of chancery*. Cambridge: Cambridge UP. Retrieved from HeinOnline.

Myers, I. B., McCauley, M., Quenk, N., & Hammer, A. (1998). *MBTI manual: A guide to the development and use of the Myers-Briggs Type Indicator Instrument* (3rd ed.). Mountain View, CA: Consulting Psychologists Press.

National Association for the Education of Young Children. (2005). *NAEYC code of ethical conduct and statement of commitment.* Washington, DC: National Association for the Education of Young Children.

Strauss, P. (n.d.). Due process. Retrieved from http://www.law.cornell.edu/wex/due_process

CHAPTER 2

Civil Rights Act of 1964. (1964, July 2). Public L. 88–352. Stat. 241.

Cohen, A. J. (1998, Sept.). Bettering your odds of not getting sued. *Child Care Exchange*, 74–78.

Head Start Standards of Conduct. 45 CFR 1304.52.

National Association for the Education of Young Children. (2005). Code of ethical conduct and statement of commitment. Retrieved from http://www.naeyc.org/files/naeyc/file/positions/PSETH05.pdf.

Podcast. Managing Risks in ECE: Preventing legal hot spots from becoming lawsuits. Retrieved from http://www.earlychildhoodwebinars.org/presentations/managing-risks-in-ece-preventing-legal-hot-spots-from-becoming-lawsuits-by-tom-copeland-and-holly-elissa-bruno

U.S. Department of Justice, Civil Rights Division. (n.d). Types of educational opportunities discrimination. Available at http://www.justice.gov/crt/about/edu/types.php

CHAPTER 3

Copeland, T. (2006). *Family child care: Contracts & policies* (3rd ed.). St. Paul, MN: Redleaf Press.

Copeland, T. (2012). *Family child care: Marketing guide* (2nd ed.). St. Paul, MN: Redleaf Press.

Minnesota Administrative Rules, 9502.0405, Subpart 4(E). Minnesota Office of the Revisor of Statutes. Retrieved from https://www.revisor.mn.gov/rules/?id=9502.0405

National Association for the Education of Young Children. (2005). Code of ethical conduct and statement of commitment. Retrieved from http://www.naeyc.org/files/naeyc/file/positions/PSETH05.pdf.

Pennsylvania Department of Public Welfare. (2010). Child care regulations. Retrieved from http://www.dpw.state.pa.us/provider/earlylearning/childcareregulations/index.htm

Sherman Antitrust Act. (1890). 15 U.S.C. §§1–7.

State of California. (2007). Child care regulations. Office of Governor Edmund G. Brown Jr. Retrieved from http://www.dss.cahwnet.gov/ord/PG587.htm

CHAPTER 4

Bloom, P. J., & Eisenberg, E. (2003, Spring–Summer). Reshaping early childhood programs to be more family responsive. *America's Family Support Magazine, 21,* 36–38.

Bowman, B., & Moore, E. K. (Eds.). (2006). *School readiness and social emotional development: Perspectives in cultural diversity.* Washington, DC: National Black Child Development Institute.

Bruno, H. E. (2003, Sept.–Oct.). Hearing parents in every language: An invitation to ECE professionals. *Child Care Exchange,* 58–60.

Bruno, H. E. (2010, May–June). "Hold harmless" option for staff babysitting and employee references. *Child Care Exchange,* 68–72.

Center for the Study of Social Policy. (2004). *Protecting children by strengthening families: A guidebook for early childhood programs.* Washington, DC: Center for the Study of Social Policy.

Child Care Law Center. (2005). Releasing children from child care and custody issues: With whom can the child go home? Retrieved from http://www.childcarelaw.org/docs/releasingchildren.pdf

Christian, L. G. (2006). Understanding families: Applying family systems theory to early childhood practice. *Young Children, 61*(1), 12–20.

Coontz, S. (1997). *The way we really are: Coming to terms with America's changing family.* New York: Perseus Books.

Gonzalez-Mena, J. (2008). *Child, family, and community: Family-centered early care and education* (5th ed.). Upper Saddle River, NJ: Pearson/Merrill/Prentice Hall.

Governors Highway Safety Association. (2012). Child passenger safety laws. Retrieved from http://www.ghsa.org/html/stateinfo/laws/childsafety_laws.html

Insurance Institute for Highway Safety. (2012). Motorcycle and bicycle helmet use laws. Retrieved from http://www.iihs.org/laws/HelmetUseCurrent.aspx#1

Keyser, J. (2006). *Building a family-centered early childhood program.* Washington, DC: National Association for the Education of Young Children.

Kugler, E. (2010). Bridging the disconnect between educational leaders and diverse families. Heart to heart conversations on leadership: Your guide to making a difference. Retrieved from http://www.bamradionetwork.com/index.php?option=com_content&view=article&id=547:jackstreet54&catid=69:infobamradionetworkcom&Itemid=144

McGuckin, R. V. (n.d.). Legal insights for the child care provider: Employee babysitting and other outside employment issues. Retrieved from http://www.naccp.org/displaycommon.cfm?an=1&subarticlenbr=538

National Association for the Education of Homeless Children and Youth. (2010, Nov.). Immigration and schools: Supporting success for undocumented and unaccompanied homeless youth. Retrieved from http://www.centrolatinoamericano.org/images/uploads/Immigrant_Youth_November_2010.pdf

National Association for the Education of Young Children. (2005). *NAEYC code of ethical conduct and statement of commitment.* Washington, DC: National Association for the Education of Young Children.

Powell, D. R. (1998). Research in review: Reweaving parents into the fabric of early childhood programs. *Young Children, 53*(5), 60–67.

Serrie, J. (2011, July 26). School officials: Alabama law on reporting illegal students is "impractical." Retrieved from http://www.foxnews.com/politics/2011/07/26/illegal-immigration-crackdown-stirs-debate-in-alabama

CHAPTER 5

American Health Association and American Academy of Pediatrics. (2011). Caring for our children: National Health and Safety Performance Standards Guidelines for early care and education programs. Retrieved from http://nrckids.org/CFOC3

Coen, J. (2006, Apr. 28). Fatal beating by dad called "torture"; father convicted in daughter's murder. *Chicago Tribune.* Retrieved from http://tinyurl.com/72rccux

Consumer Product Safety Commission. (2008, April). *Public playground safety handbook.* Bethesda, MD: Consumer Product Safety Commission.

Copeland, T., & Millard, M. (2004). *Family child care: Legal & insurance guide.* St. Paul, MN: Redleaf Press.

Fisher, M. C. (2005). *American Academy of Pediatrics: Immunizations and infectious diseases.* American Academy of Pediatrics

National Association for Child Care Resource and Referral Agencies. (2011). Emergency preparedness for child care: A how-to guide. Retrieved from http://www.naccrra.org/publications/naccrra-publications/2011/12/emergency-preparedness-for-child-care-a-how-to-guide

National Conference of State Legislatures. (2010, Nov.). Sudden infant death syndrome (SIDS). Retrieved from http://www.ncsl.org/issues-research/health/sudden-infant-death-syndrome-laws.aspx

National Conference of State Legislatures. (2012, Jan.). States with religious and philosophical exemptions from school immunization requirements. Retrieved from http://www.ncsl.org/issues-research/health/school-immunization-exemption-state-laws.aspx

Olson, R. (2008, May 30). Court gets behind spanking, to a degree. *Star Tribune.* Retrieved from http://www.corpun.com/usd00805.htm

Public Health Law Center. (2011). Smoke-free child care: A policy overview. Retrieved from http://publichealthlawcenter.org/sites/default/files/resources/phlc-fs-smokefreechildcare-2011.pdf

CHAPTER 6

American Academy of Pediatrics. (2011). *Caring for our children: National health and safety performance standards: Guidelines for early care and early education programs* (3rd ed.). Elk Grove Village, IL: American Academy of Pediatrics.

American Civil Liberties Union. (2002, Dec. 6). How the USA Patriot Act defines "domestic terrorism." Retrieved from http://www.aclu.org/national-security/how-usa-patriot-act-redefines-domestic-terrorism

Americans with Disabilities Act of 1990 (ADA). (1990). 42 U.S.C. sec. 12101.

Anctil, J. (2011). SAU #39 ESOL compliance manual. Milford, New Hampshire, School Administrative District #39. Retrieved from http://sprise.com/special.aspx?id=794

Borg, J. (2008). *Body language: 7 easy lessons to master the silent language.* Upper Saddle River, NJ: Pearson Education.

Bruno, H. E. (2010, Jan.–Feb.). Creating relational sanctuaries for children who suffer from abuse. *Child Care Exchange,* 64–68.

Center for American Progress. (2011, Oct. 27). All children matter: CAP event discusses how legal and social inequalities hurt LGBT families. Retrieved from http://www.americanprogress.org/issues/2011/10/all_children_matter_writeup.html

Defense of Marriage Act (DOMA). (1996). Public Law 104-199, H.R. 3396, 104th Cong.

Ford, J. (2009). *Hotel on the corner of bitter and sweet.* New York: Ballantine Books.

Gay and Lesbian Alliance against Defamation (GLAAD). (2010). Frequently asked questions: Defense of Marriage Act. Retrieved from http://www.glaad.org/resources/doma

Individuals with Disabilities Education Improvement Act of 2004 (Public Law 108-446, H.R. 1350, 108th Cong.). (2004).

Kissen, R. (Ed.). (2003). *Getting ready for Benjamin: Preparing teachers for sexual diversity in the classroom.* New York: Rowman & Littlefield Publishers.

Lazarus, E. (1883). The new colossus. Unpublished sonnet displayed on the Statue of Liberty. It was engraved on a plaque for the statue in 1903.

Lipkin, A. (2003). *Beyond diversity day: A Q&A on gay and lesbian issues in schools.* New York: Rowman & Littlefield Publishers.

MacGillivray, I. (2004). *Sexual orientation and school policy: A practical guide for teachers, administrators and community activists.* Oxford, UK: Rowland & Littlefield.

Movement Advancement Project. (2012). Snapshot: LGBT legal equality by state. Retrieved from http://www.lgbtmap.org/equality-maps/legal_equality_by_state

National Association for the Education of Young Children. (2005). *NAEYC code of ethical conduct and statement of commitment.* Washington, DC: National Association for the Education of Young Children.

Nemeth, K. (2012). *Many languages, building connections: Supporting infants and toddlers who are dual-language learners.* Lewisville, NC: Gryphon House.

Omer, S. (2012, Feb. 8). In school sex scandal, parents fear deportation if they talk. Retrieved from http://usnews.msnbc.msn.com/_news/2012/02/08/10355458-in-school-sex-scandal-parents-fear-deportation-if-they-talk

Rehabilitation Act of 1973, Section 504, 29 U.S.C. sec. 794. (2000).

Richardson, J., & Parnell, P. (2005). *And tango makes three.* New York: Simon & Shuster.

S. 1125–112th Congress (2011). USA PATRIOT Act Improvements Act of 2011. Retrieved from http://www.govtrack.us/congress/bill.xpd?bill= s112-1125

Schimmel, D., Eckes, S., & Militello, M. (2010). *Principals teaching the law: Ten legal questions your teachers must know.* Thousand Oaks, CA: Corwin.

Soennichsen, J. (2011). *The Chinese Exclusion Act of 1882.* Santa Barbara, CA: Greenwood.

U.S. Department of Education. (2012, Jan. 10). Laws enforced by Office of Civil Rights (OCR). Retrieved from http://www2.ed.gov/about/offices/list/ocr/complaints-how.html

U.S. Equal Employment Opportunity Commission. (1993). *Americans with Disabilities Act handbook.* Washington, DC: Author.

USA Patriot Act. (2001). Public Law 107-56. 115 Stat. 272.

Wessler, S. F. (2012, Feb. 14). Deported dad begs North Carolina to give him back his children. Retrieved from http://colorlines.com/archives/2012/deported_dad_begs_north_carolina_not_put_kids_into_adoption.html

Wood, K. I., & Youcha, V. (2009). *The ABCs of the ADA: Your early childhood program's guide to the Americans with Disabilities Act.* Baltimore, MD: Brookes.

Yell, M. (2006). *The law and special education.* Upper Saddle River, NJ: Pearson Prentice Hall.

Youngblood, L. A. (2011, Nov. 3). Antimarriage equality laws often affect children most. Retrieved from http://secular.org/blogs/lauren-anderson-youngblood/anti-marriage-equality laws-often-affect-children-most

CHAPTER 7

Copeland, T., & Millard, M. (2004). *Family child care: Legal & insurance guide.* St. Paul, MN: Redleaf Press.

Data Quality Campaign. (n.d.). Federal privacy laws applicable to early childhood education. Federal laws. Retrieved from http://dataquality campaign.org:8080/build/legal_guide/federal_laws/childhood

Performance review confidentiality. (2010, June 15). Human Resources Blog. Retrieved from http://www.humanresourceblog.com/2010/06/15/performance-review-confidentiality

CHAPTER 8

Adler, L. (2007). *Hire with your head: Using performance-based hiring to build great teams.* Hoboken, NJ: John Wiley & Sons.

Bowman, L. (2011). Americans with Disabilities Act as Amended: Principles and practice. *New Directions for Adult and Continuing Education,* 85–95.

Bruno, H. E. (2005, Sept.–Oct.). At the end of the day: Legal and ethical issues at release time. *Child Care Exchange,* 66–69.

Bruno, H. E. (2010, May–June). "Hold harmless" option for staff babysitting and employee references. *Child Care Exchange*, 68–72.

Bruno, H. E., & Batiste, L. C. (2010). Sweeping new definitions of disabilities: What you need to know. Retrieved from http://www.bamradionetwork.com/index.php?option=com_content&view=article&id=580:jackstreet54&catid=36:administrators-channel&Itemid=90

Cannice v. Northwest Bank, Iowa, N.A., 189 F.3d 723 (8th Cir. 1999).

Child Care Law Center. (1996). *Employing people with disabilities: The Americans with Disabilities Act and child care.* San Francisco, CA: Child Care Law Center.

Civil Rights Act of 1964. (1964, July 2). Public L. 88–352. Stat. 241.

Copeland, T., & Millard, M. (2004). *Family child care: Legal & insurance guide.* St. Paul, MN: Redleaf Press.

Michigan Family Independence Agency. (2004, Spring). Michigan Child Care Matters (64). Retrieved from http://www.michigan.gov/documents/fia_ocal_mccm67_86588_7.pdf

Murray, C. S. (1988). Compelled self-publication in the employment context: A consistent exception to the defamation requirement of publication. *Washington and Lee Law Review*, 45(1).

National Association for the Education of Young Children. (n.d.). NAEYC accreditation criteria/quality standards. Retrieved from http://www.cde.state.co.us/cpp/download/QualityStandards/naeycQualityStandardsCrosswalk.pdf

U.S. Department of Justice. (2000). Federal protections against national origin discrimination. Available at http://www.justice.gov/crt/legalinfo/natorigin.php

CHAPTER 9

Americans with Disabilities Act Amendments Act of 2008 (ADAAA). (2008, July 31). Public L. 110–325. Stat. 3406.

Bruce, S. (2011, March 28). Probationary periods—Dangerous device or necessary tool? HR Daily Advisor. Retrieved from http://hrdailyadvisor.blr.com/archive/2011/03/28/Hiring_Recruiting_Policies_Probationary_Periods.aspx

Bruno, H. E. (2007, Sept.). Gossip free zones: Problem solving to prevent power struggles. *Young Children*.

Bruno, H. E. (2010a). Curtailing high turnover among early childhood educators. Heart to heart conversations on leadership: Your guide to making a difference. Retrieved from http://www.bamradionetwork.com/index.php?option=com_content&view=category&layout=blog&id=49&Itemid=81&limitstart=8

Bruno, H. E. (2010b). Gossip: Small talk, big impact on classrooms and children. Heart to heart conversations on leadership: Your guide to making a difference. Retrieved from http://www.bamradionetwork.com/index.php?option=com_content&view=article&id=237:jack1&catid=36:administrators-channel&Itemid=90

Bruno, H. E. (2010c). Silencing the whiners on your staff. Retrieved from http:// www.jackstreet.com/jackstreet/WNHSA.Bruno.cfm

Bruno, H. E. (2011, July–Aug.). Eliminate whining in the workplace: Moving beyond "grin and bear it." *Child Care Exchange,* 93–96.

Bruno, H. E. (2012a). Three steps to encourage ECE teachers to be problem solvers: Encourage winners, not whiners! Early Childhood Investigations. Retrieved from http://www.earlychildhoodwebinars.org/presentations/ ece-directors-you-want-staff-winners-not-whiners-3-steps-to-create-a-staff-of-problem-solvers

Bruno, H. E. (2012b). *What you need to lead an early childhood program: Emotional intelligence in practice.* Washington, DC: NAEYC.

Connors, N. (2000). *If you don't feed the teachers they eat the students: Guide to success for administrators and teachers.* Nashville, TN: Incentive Publications.

Cornell University Law School. (2012). *Employment discrimination.* Ithaca, NY: Legal Information Institute. Retrieved from http://www.law.cornell .edu/wex/employment_discrimination

Cozolino, L. (2006). *The neuroscience of human relationships: Attachment and the developing social brain.* New York: W. W. Norton & Company.

D'Cruz, J. (n.d.). Documentation, discipline, and discharge. Morris, Manning & Martin, LLP. Retrieved from http://www.mmmlaw.com/media-room/ publications/articles/documentation-discipline-and-discharge

Freedom of Information Act (FOIA). (1966). 5 U.S.C. § 55.

Goleman, D. (2011). *The brain and emotional intelligence: New insights.* Northampton, MA: More Than Sound LLC.

Guerin, L., & DelPo, A. (n.d.). Keeping personnel files and medical records confidential. Retrieved from http://www.nolo.com/legal-encyclopedia/ keeping-personnel-files-medical-records-confidential-29777.html

Health Insurance Portability and Accountability Act of 1996 (HIPPA). (1996). 110 Stat. 1936.

HIPPA World Privacy Forum. (2009). A patient's guide to HIPAA part 3: What you should know about uses and disclosures. Retrieved from http:// worldprivacyforum.org/hipaa/HipaaGuidePart3.html

Legal Information Institute. (n.d.). Employment discrimination. Cornell University Law School. Retrieved from http://www.law.cornell.edu/wex/ employment_discrimination

McDaniel, M. A. (2007). Progressive discipline policies and employment at will. Retrieved from http://www.bickerstaff.com/files/MAM_Progressive _Discipline_4_17_07.pdf

Montana Code. Ann. Sec. 39-2-904 (2008).

National Association for the Education of Young Children. (2005). Code of ethical conduct and statement of commitment. Retrieved from http://www .naeyc.org/files/naeyc/file/positions/PSETH05.pdf

Onder, A. (2009, Jan. 16). 3rd Circuit: Anxiety and depression not evidence of ADA disability. Retrieved from http://www.shrm.org/LegalIssues/ FederalResources/Pages/dCircuitAnxietyandDepressionNotEvidenceof ADADisability.aspx

Schimelpfening, N. (2012, Feb. 7). The Americans with Disabilities Act and you. Retrieved from http://depression.about.com/cs/disability/a/ada.htm

West Virginia Employment Law Letter. (2008, Apr. 8). What can HR do about workplace gossip? Retrieved from http://www.hrhero.com/hl/articles/2008/04/04/what-can-hr-do-about-workplace-gossip

Wrongful Discharge from Employment Act (WDEA). (2008). Montana Code Ann. Sec. 39-2-904.

CHAPTER 10

Copeland, T., & Millard, M. (2004). *Family child care: Legal & insurance guide.* St. Paul, MN: Redleaf Press.

U.S. Small Business Administration. (n.d.) Insurance. Retrieved from http://www.sba.gov/category/navigation-structure/starting-managing-business/managing-business/running-business/insurance

Volker, C. (1992). *Liability insurance and the child care center.* NCR Extension Publication No. 434. Ames, IA: Iowa State University Extension. Available at http://www.nncc.org/Business/liabil.ins.ccc.html#anchor350406

Index

About the Authors

Holly Elissa Bruno, MA, JD, is an author, keynote speaker, and radio host at BAM radio. She teaches leadership and management courses for Wheelock College. She served as assistant attorney general for the state of Maine and assistant dean at the University of Maine School of Law. She can be reached at www.hollyelissabruno.com.

Tom Copeland, JD, is a trainer and advocate for the business of child care. He has written nine books on the business of family child care. He trains tax professionals and trainers and has successfully represented child care providers in U.S. Tax Court. His blog, www.tomcopelandblog.com, is a leading source of information on the business of child care.